7 Laws

of

black Hair

Also by Toyosi Onwuemene

My Hair is Beauty

Toyosi Onwuemene

7 Laws

of

black Hair

Uncover the Principles that Govern *black* Hair Glory

Onwuemene Publishing Group
Raleigh, North Carolina
MM XVIII

This book is dedicated to *black* hair.
You are an instrument of worship; a symbol of beauty, resilience, strength, and grace. May you fulfill your ultimate destiny on the heads of the ones graced by your presence. And may you live each day basking in the glory of the One who makes you truly beautiful.

Contents

Acknowledgments

This project was made possible by the support of the wonderful people in my life. It is my life's greatest pleasure to be surrounded by friends and family who encourage me to fulfill my dreams. So many of you cheered me on to the successful completion of this book that I have, unfortunately, left out more names than I included. I ask forgiveness of all whose names are not shown here. Know that your names are indelibly written on the pages of my heart.

To the Ancient One. You light up my life with goodness. Thank You for bringing this book to life. I have so much to learn from You as I aspire to Your creativity. Thank You for teaching me. Thank You for helping me accomplish everything You have called me to do.

To Chiedu, who always inspires me to do better. I admire your can-do attitude and strong work ethic. Watching you get up and go every day, no matter the circumstance, inspires me to cast my worries aside and just do it.

To Jonathan, for being the first to make me question who and what I live for. I enjoy your warm smile, sweet spirit, and inquisitive mind. Conversation with you is a delight.

To Joelle, for being the inspiration behind this book. Thank you for causing me to stop and think about what is truly important to me about my own hair.

To Mom and Dad. Thank you for naming me Oluwatoyosi. I bask in the beauty and glory of that name daily. Eniti o nyọ s'Oluwa l'ọrun ni mo jẹ. Oluwa si kẹ mi. Ẹṣe.

To my other Mom and Dad. You loved me from the first

day you met me, and have kept loving me since. Thank you!

To Ife, Adeolu, and Tokunbo, the "fires" that forged me. What would I have become without you? You inspire me to greatness. I couldn't have asked for a better team.

To Renardo, Oluchi, Gandhi, Awele, and Uchenna. I really lucked out. Thank you for everything you do behind the scenes to bring joy to my life.

To Uncle Sunny and Ngozi. I am left speechless at your sacrifice. Thank you for believing I would make it.

To Kayla, Natalie, Ama, Seun, Lauryn, Gracie, Cece, and every young lady who will make a decision to embrace her own black hair. May you find the courage to discover what is most unique and special about you.

To Isaiah, Jed, Austin, Ethan, Gabriel, Nathanael, and Evan. May you find grace to encourage the ladies in your life to find their True North.

To Mrs. T, for coming with me on this incredible journey. You are a fantastic educator, hair doctor, and friend. Thank you for believing I would bring this dream to pass.

To Ms. April. You inspire me to greatness. Thank you for your great vision to give young girls true love for their hair.

To Cinnamon. I share ideas with you and they come to life. Thank you for letting me share.

To Tom, you give me permission to think outside the box. You listen and have great ideas. You have your own unique hair story and I appreciate you for living it daily.

To Benedict and Emmanuela, thank you for helping me bring this great vision to pass. You stepped in at just the right time and were willing to share your gifts with me. Thank you.

To Pastors Bisi and Toyin. I blossom under your leadership. Thank you for helping me to thrive in all my gifts.

To Pastors Kim and Martha. I love and miss you dearly.

To the incredible team at Onwuemene Publishing Group. You are amazing! Thank you for the sleepless nights in the final push through to bring this book to reality. Look at what you did! Thank you!

Preface
(Or frequently asked questions)

How Do You Define *black* Hair?
For the purposes of this book, *black* hair is defined as hair that, in its natural, unaltered, unprocessed state, grows upwards and outwards. It refers to hair that does not naturally hang down-wards but, rather, stands tall in defiance of gravity. *black* hair typically characterizes, but is not unique to, the dark- (or relatively dark-) skinned people of the African diaspora whose hair type is tightly coiled or curly.

Why *black* Rather Than Black Hair?
I use the lowercase, rather than uppercase, "b" to denote *black* hair because I feel it necessary to distinguish between *black* hair type and Black race. Some Black people do not have *black* hair and some people with *black* hair are not Black. Overall, more Black people have *black* hair than do not. Nevertheless, I am careful to make this distinction because the correlation between *black* hair and Black people is not 100%. Additionally, I use the lowercase "b" for dramatic effect.

Why Write About Only One Hair Type?
The principles outlined in this book are not exclusive to *black* hair and can be broadly applied to other hair types. Furthermore, beyond hair, the laws can be metaphorically applied to other aspects of life. Nevertheless, the principles outlined in this book are tailored to *black* hair. My focus is *black* hair because it is a unique and distinct hair type that is sometimes ostracized, often politicized, and frequently misunderstood. Many books have been written about other hair types. Therefore, this book has been written specially to honor *black* hair.

Can I Read This Book If Don't Have *black* Hair?

If you do not have *black* hair, allow me to express my sincere appreciation for your willingness to read this book. Yes, this book is also for you because most of the principles outlined in it are applicable to your hair type. This book is also for you because you likely know and interact with one or more persons with *black* hair and this book will give you some tools to help encourage a friend along her *black* hair journey.

Can Men Also Read This Book?

Although I wrote this book with a female audience in mind, the principles outlined in it are also applicable to men. This book is relevant to men with or without *black* hair who desire to support the *black*-haired women in their lives. Therefore, if you are a man reading this book, welcome. Thank you for reading. Please note that, whenever I refer to *black* hair with the personal pronoun, "she," you are free to substitute the masculine "he," as desired.

Introduction

Your head of curls is defiant. It breaks norms, hates boundaries, refuses to be tamed, talks back, defies gravity, and stands tall. Your mane breaks rules, won't read books, can't follow instructions, and won't lay low. Your coils are unruly to the point of frustration! So frustrating are they, that you resign, throw in the towel, give up, let go, sell out, cover up, and hide. And, like the proverbial black sheep of the family, your glorious hair stays hidden, out of sight, not talked about, invisible.

Your hair doesn't live up to expectations. Not your expectations and certainly not the world's. Many times, your attempts to wear your own hair are laughed at. Instead of compliments, you receive insults. In place of praise, you experience mockery. These negative experiences can be demoralizing. Why should the way your hair was naturally created be a source of shame? It may not be for you; but for many people with *black* hair, it is. And for this reason, I write this book.

I write this book to take away the stigma that has become attached to your scrunched up, coiled, knotty, and easily tangled hair. I write because there are not enough books written about *black* hair. I write because I once looked to find validation in a book that no one had yet written. I write for future generations of women who will find courage to start their little girls off on the right *black* hair journey. I write for those little girls who will buck tradition and create a new hair path for themselves. I write for the people who don't get it, who don't understand why your hair "looks like that!" I write because you are created in the image of an incredible God whose beauty could not be captured in one look, so He created many different pictures of His glory, as represented in you. I write because you are beautiful, and you deserve to live in the glorious fullness of your beauty. The beauty you first had before the worlds were formed. I write for You.

This book is the key to unlocking the desire and passion for your hair that already lives inside you. You secretly think your hair can be beautiful, but you don't know how to make it work. You have tried hairstyles that you have regretted because someone gave you "the look" or said something disparaging. You think everyone, except you, has "good hair." Well, look no further, this book is for you. This book will change the way you think about your *black* hair. Changing the way you think about your hair is the first step to unlocking the secrets of your beautiful, luscious, glorious, head of curls.

This book is not a how-to guide. You will find no step-by-step instructions here. There are no details on how to style your hair or maintain your do. Fortunately, many books, magazines, Online websites, and articles already do that. Rather, this book will focus simply on the most important principles that define your *black* hair's glory.

Now, are you ready to start your journey to unlocking the secrets to the most beautiful asset you have? Yes, I am talking about your hair! No, not your sister's or your best friend's or your boss's. Yours! Find a comfortable spot and prepare your mind to receive new information. I will be your guide on this journey. Let's go!

Your *black* Hair

A Hair Story

One of the most important hair stories I ever heard told is the story of a woman named Mary.[1] Mary was not like most women. Where most women were accepted in their communities, Mary was avoided. Everyone avoided her because she had a dark past.

Everyone knew her story. It was the one all the neighbors talked about. It was a story mothers told their daughters as a cautionary tale. They warned their daughters, "stay away from Mary." Mary was the one to whom people gave a knowing look as she passed by. No one would speak to her. They mostly spoke around her, about her, above her, across her, but never directly to her. Mary knew her past and was eager to put it behind her. The problem is that no one would let her forget.

One day, Mary's life changed. She committed an act of love. It was an act so profound, no one would ever forget it. In fact, what she did forever changed the way people saw spoke about her. From the moment she did it, they would no longer identify her by her sordid past. What she did was an act of love that would become her new story. And what was this act? She met a Man named Jesus, poured expensive perfume on His feet, and wiped His feet with her hair.

Say what? Exactly what I said. She took her snotty-nosed face (did I mention she was crying?) and wiped His feet with her hair. Sounds crazy, doesn't it? That's exactly what the eyewitnesses thought. They thought she had lost it. I imagine someone in the room may have said, "I always knew she was crazy, but she's gone and done it now!" Mr. Moneybags, who was also in the room, said, "What a waste of money." Another guy, let's call Him "Mr. Preacher," looked down at her in disgust. "Thank God it's not me she's touching. Yuck!"

But what about the One whose feet she had cleaned with her hair? What did He have to say about it? He saw her crazy, out-of-this-world, unacceptable behavior as an act of worship.

Let's think about this point for a minute. You may not be religious, but you certainly know what it means to worship. Does your image of worship fit with the picture of a woman using her hair to wipe someone's feet? The image itself seems kind of awkward. I imagine myself in Mary's place. My 'fro may be tall; but it's still just a 'fro. I would have had to contort my neck and twist it around just right to get at His feet. I may have been able to wipe a tear or two but I'm not sure I could have accomplished much more without breaking my neck.

You're thinking "Yeah right! Mary probably had "good hair." The kind of good hair that cascades down your back and billows in the wind. The kind of good hair that is luscious and beautiful. The kind of hair that you long for. The one you don't have.

Stay with me for a minute. Mary worshiped with her hair. Until that time, no one had ever done that for Jesus. In fact, no one had ever done anything like that before. People were always washing feet; but no one had ever used their own hair to do it. Mary used her hair in an act of extravagant worship. It was such an act as to be unforgettable. From that moment on, when people referred to her, she became "That Mary" who did the thing with her hair.[2]

Let's think about the qualities of Mary's hair that may have contributed to her being able to use it as an instrument of worship.

Think about the following 5 things: 1) Her hair was long (or her neck very flexible); 2) Her hair was healthy; 3) She didn't consider what other people would say about her hair; 4) She used her hair to meet an important need; and 5) She got dirty (I'll bet that day, Jesus had pretty dirty feet).

Let's examine these 5 points:

Her Hair was Long. All hair grows long. I don't need to sell this point to you because you know it to be true. Try keeping the same hairstyle for 3 weeks. By the end of the 3rd week, there is an underbrush of thick hair that sometimes makes you wish your hair didn't grow at all. So, I'm going to believe that you know that your hair grows daily. Then, you also know that hair growth is not your problem. If I have sold you on the fact that your hair can and does grow, then you may then realize that poor retention, not poor growth, is the real problem. Keep this thought in mind: Your hair can and does grow long. Long hair worships. In chapter 4, we will talk about the Law of Retention and the rules that govern retaining your God-given long hair.

Her Hair was Healthy. We know Mary's hair was healthy because it was absorbent. It was absorbent enough to wipe away tears. You can substitute absorbent with another word like permeable, porous, or spongy. Your hair is like a sponge. She loves moisture; but she struggles to hold on to it. In chapter 5, the Law of Moisture, we will learn about the importance of moisturizing your hair. But suffice it for now to say that hair that is not moisturized is brittle. Brittle hair is unhealthy hair that is characterized by breakage. Brittle and breakable hair does not worship well. For your hair to be worship-ready, it must be healthy. If it's not healthy, it must be nursed back to health.

She Didn't Consider What Other People Would Say About Her Hair. Let's face it, not everyone will like your hair. Truth be told, they don't like it whatever you do. As long as you cover it up, hide it in extensions, braids, a wig, or something, it's OK. But let them see your natural curly 'fro and they freak out. You're in trouble if you do and in trouble if you don't. Look, give up worrying! The moment you give up worrying about what your friends and the neighbors think about your hair is the moment you become free to release her to worship with abandon. Only by letting go can you truly worship. It is interesting to note that the moment you let go of people's thoughts and judgments about your hair, you begin to live in a place of hair beauty that brings people to admire you. Imagine that! The same people who told you your hair was ugly would now like to know how to achieve the look you have. The key is to take your eyes off people as the source of your self-validation. If your hair is to be a source of worship, the one to validate her as worthy is you. Realize that her Maker has already validated her. Your validation is the one she awaits, the one she strongly craves. Please validate her and then release her to worship.

She Used Her Hair to Meet a Need. Mary didn't think much of her needs. In fact, she thought the most about Jesus's needs. "What could she give Him?" She wondered. What could she do for Him? When she considered it long and hard, she realized His feet were dirty and they needed cleaning. She decided that she would clean His feet and she washed them as an act of service. But why didn't she use a towel? Surely, someone in the room had even a handkerchief that she could have used. I bet her dress was long enough that she could have used its hem to wipe His feet. But if she did that, it would not have been extraordinary. For it to be extraordinary, she used something that was precious. She used the part of her body that was most glorious. She used her hair. She effectively said to Jesus, "You have a need, and I will use my most glorious possession to meet that need. I will use my hair to tell you how much you mean to me." In her act of worship, she used her hair to meet a need.

Similarly, as an instrument of worship, your hair meets needs. Yes, she makes you look beautiful; but beyond that, she inspires. Every time you wear your *black* hair beautifully and proudly, someone else is encouraged. A young girl looks at you and knows that, because your hair is beautiful, her hair must be beautiful too. Think about what it says to a generation of little girls with *black* hair who don't get to see their own hair represented in daily life. If, every time they see *black* hair, it is wrapped up in a weave, covered up in extensions, or folded up in a wig, what does that say to them about the beauty and glory of their own hair. Every time you wear your hair as an act of worship, you meet the needs of people around you. You meet their need to see your *black* hair look gorgeous.

She Got Dirty. Should you choose, like Mary, to use your hair as an act of worship, you will get "dirty." Getting dirty means that it will cost you. It may cost you time and money. You may have to let go of your preconceived ideas about what your hair should look like. You may have to dismantle existing cultural norms. You may even have to let go of your current, established, hair reputation. But whatever you do, if your hair will truly worship, it will cost you. Hair that will worship requires that a price be paid. Your hair will only achieve its greatest glory in the place of your biggest sacrifice.

I personally believe that the beauty of your hair is revealed in its ultimate act of service to the One who made you (whether or not you acknowledge His presence). I believe that to demonstrate the lavish beauty of your hair is to demonstrate His infinite wisdom in creating her. To allow your hair to be her best, most beautiful self, is to tell of His love. To allow your hair to thrive in a way that makes heads turn is to reflect His glory. Your hair is made in His hair's image and likeness and, to realize her true potential, you must abandon her to worship. She really does desire to worship. Don't hold her back.

An Introduction to the 7 Laws

I invite you to consider that your hair is really His hair. His expression of His creativity, His delight, and His humor, revealed in you. Your hair is His hair. And, if His hair is your hair, then consider how you are representing His hair in your Hair. For your hair to become all that she was created to be, you must unlock her secrets.

In the next 7 chapters, these secrets will be discussed. These secrets are not truly secrets, but rather principles. Principles that, until now, have not been uniformly applied to your hair. These principles are also known as laws.

According to the Merriam Webster Online Dictionary, a law is defined as "a rule of conduct formally recognized as binding or enforced by a controlling authority."[3] Laws are secrets when people don't know what they are.

Unfortunately, whether or not you acknowledge their existence, laws apply to you. As long as you live, you are subject to the law.

The act of breaking the law confers the same consequences on both the ignorant and the informed. Becoming informed about the law sets you free to choose your own outcomes intentionally. Knowing the law sets you free to choose. Wise choices come from understanding the laws that govern us. Wise choices about your *black* hair can only come from understanding her governing laws.

Recognize that there are many laws that govern your *black* hair. In this book, I discuss only 7. The 7 laws that I will discuss in the remaining chapters of this book, are as follows:

1. The Law of Love: What you love thrives.

2. The Law of Investment: Every investment will bring a return.

3. The Law of Retention: You keep what you retain.

4. The Law of Moisture: What is brittle will break.

5. The Law of Protection: Weaknesses are to be protected.

6. The Law of Investigation: What is not investigated is misunderstood.

7. The Law of Exposure: What people don't see, they don't know.

As we study these laws, consider how they apply to you in your daily interactions with your hair. Consider how a new understanding of these laws can change your experience of your hair and transform the way she looks.

Let us begin.

The Law of Love

What You Love Thrives

The Law of Love

The Law of Love states that, when you actively love your hair, she will thrive.

Definitions

The Merriam-Webster Dictionary defines "love" and "thrive" in ways that are relevant to our discussion as follows:

Love[1]

1. Strong affection for another arising out of kinship or personal ties.

2. Affection based on admiration.

3. Unselfish loyal and benevolent concern for the good of another.

Thrive[2]

1. To grow vigorously

2. To grow or develop successfully

3. To flourish or succeed

From the above definitions, we can reword the Law of Love in the following way:

When you actively show strong affection for and unselfish loyal and benevolent concern for the good of your hair, she will grow vigorously, develop successfully, flourish, and succeed.

I Didn't Love my *black* Hair

I don't know when it happened; but one day, I woke up and realized that I didn't love my *black* hair. How could I love it? It was springy, curly, tightly-coiled, stiff, it stood on end. What kind of hair did I have and where did it come from? I was surrounded by so many people with long, flowing hair. Hair that billowed in the wind. My hair? It would take a gale-force wind to bend my hair even an inch. What was wrong with me? Why was I born with "inferior" hair? Or so I thought. Why would God do this to me?

These were questions that stayed with me from childhood through adulthood. I couldn't understand my hair. And each time I tried to "fix" it, it wouldn't cooperate. Nothing I tried seemed right. For years, I tried different natural hairstyles, most of which I didn't like. And, when I finally found one I liked, invariably, I came across someone who didn't like it. So then, because someone else didn't like it, I didn't like it either. I had enough of these experiences that, ultimately, I hated my own hair.

I hated my own hair but was stuck with it. I felt compelled to stick with it. However, I needed to try something different. Not permanent, but different. From the looks of so many beautiful women around me, that different thing would have to be to wear it straight. Straight hair appeared to be the nirvana that all women were meant to achieve. I was an adult but had never had the experience of getting my natural hair temporarily straightened. So, one day, I decided I would do it! I would go get my hair straightened. I would get my hair "pressed."

Well, press my hair they did, and boy, was it beautiful. It was long, silky, and fluffy. It even billowed in the wind (this was Chicago in the Fall). I thought I looked pretty cool. But I was not prepared for the reaction:

Everyone loved it. Everyone! My husband, my friends, my co-workers . . . Everyone, but me. They gushed over my hair and told me it was beautiful. They gave me so many compliments that I was sick to my stomach. How could they all gush over this silky, straight, long, flowing hair? Hair that was not really mine? I hated it! I hated it because it wasn't me. I hated it because I felt my hair was telling a lie. It wasn't the hair I knew and loved. And, why didn't my own hair, in its natural state, elicit the same gushy, glowing, "Oh you are so gorgeous," response?" Why did people wait until my hair looked so different to acknowledge its beauty? It was the last time I would ever pursue a look I hated to secure the admiration of the people I loved.

Eventually, I found a "natural" hairstylist. Finding a natural hair stylist marked the beginning of the best days of my hair life. Once I saw what, in her natural state, my hair could do, I fell in love with her as if for the first time. I saw her in a new light. She twisted beautifully. When done in two-strand twists, she could actually billow in the (Chicago) wind. When wrapped tightly around "Flexi" rods, she came out with a nice curly look. I was introduced, in an amazing way, to the beauty and glory of my own hair, as if for the first time. And for the first time, I knew that I would love her forever. And would you know it, she loved me back.

Thou Shalt Love Your Hair

Your hair is you. You are your hair. You were created with her. She is an inherent part of your God-given beauty. To love her is to love yourself. To love yourself is to accept every part of you, including your hair. Without loving your hair, your self-love is incomplete. Yes, truly loving her as you love and accept every other part of your body is necessary. Your hair knows exactly how you feel. You say you love her, but she barely sees the light of day. You say you love her, but every time you step out in public, you cover her up. You say you love her but, rather than wear your own tresses, you choose to wear a wig. Your hair questions your love for her and so do I.

Where is Your Hair Love?

How can you love something so much and yet be ashamed of it? "I'm not ashamed!" I hear you say. Then prove it to me. When you love someone, you spend time with them, talk to them, take care of them, and talk to others about them. When you love someone, you don't need to announce it. It's in the way you walk, the way you talk, the way your eyes light up, the way you can't seem to get away, the way the time passes by when you're together. When you love someone, you show them off, take them out, show them the town. When you love someone, you're not afraid to be seen together. When you love someone, you want the world to know. Tell me, does this describe your relationship with your hair? Do you really love her? Is she an intricate part of your interactions with others? Do you show her off? Are you excited when you talk about her? Do you talk about her? Do you talk to her? Do you love her? Do you love your hair? What's important is not what you say, it's what you do.

The following are some signs that may indicate that your hair love falls short:

1. No one at work knows what your real hair looks like.

2. You would rather wear a wig than leave your hair out.

3. You are in trouble if your hairstylist cancels.

4. You have no idea how to style your own hair.

5. The hair you buy gets more compliments than the hair you were born with.

6. You have canceled going to an event because of your hair.

7. Your hair has never seen the rainbow.

8. If you came in to work wearing your own hair, your boss might not recognize you.

9. The thought of styling your own hair creates knots in your stomach.

10. You wish you were born with a different hair texture.

If most of the above statements resonate with you, it may be a sign that your hair love meter is low. But if the above statements do not describe you, then you may have cultivated strong hair love. You can tell your hair love is strong if most of the following statements apply to you.

1. It's not the end of the world if your hairstylist cancels an appointment.

2. You are not afraid of getting caught in the rain.

3. The hair you were born with gets more compliments than the hair you buy.

4. Your coworkers know what your real hair looks like.

5. You look at your hair in the mirror and like what you see.

6. You find ways to express yourself in your creative hairstyles.

7. Wearing a wig is something you do out of choice and not out of necessity.

8. An ignorant comment about your hair doesn't derail your day.

9. You know exactly what to do with a bad hair job.

10. You wear your hair as if it were a crown (because it is).

If the statements above resonate with you, it is a sign that you have a healthy dose of hair love. If, however, your hair love is lacking, don't despair. Love is an active verb. It can be cultivated. It can be grown. Let's look at some ways to grow your hair love.

Tips for Growing Hair Love

Be patient. As a result of your natural hair curliness, your hair gets easily tangled. Tangled hair should be handled with care. Each time you comb out a braid or take out a twist, spend some time to untangle it. While it is easier to just cut out the tangle, comb through it vigorously, or snap it off, stop! Take a deep breath. Do it again. Commit to investing as much time in your hair as needed to get the tangles out without hurting her. Be gentle.

Be kind to your hair. Your hair needs your kindness. To be kind is to be friendly, generous, and considerate. Think about your hair needs and satisfy them. Think about her dislikes and avoid them. Think about her feelings and be considerate. Never be caught saying something about her that you wouldn't want said about you. Don't team up with anyone to say negative things about her. Be a friend and defend her. Be an ally and nurture her. Be a companion and spend time with her. Be kind to your hair.

Take pride in your hair. Your hair is your pride and joy; own it! She is the only hair you have; wear her proudly. She is specially created for you; show her off. Her texture is unique to you; display her gloriously. No one else has hair exactly like yours; showcase her beauty. No one will give your hair more honor than you do. If you don't take pride in her, no one else will. In fact, when you speak disparagingly about your hair, you give other people the wrong language with which to address you. Speak about your hair the way you want people to speak about you. Remember, you may make a distinction between your hair and the rest of your body; but no one else makes this distinction. If you speak negatively about one aspect of your body, it is the same as speaking negatively about your entire self.

Celebrate someone else's locks. Everyone is created uniquely. Each person has unique strengths and weaknesses. Your hair is the best hair for you in the same way that their hair is the best hair for them. Whenever you look at someone else's hair, rather than get jealous, celebrate. Every time you celebrate someone else's locks, you really celebrate your own. Every time you compliment someone else's hair, you show that you value your own hair. Noticing beautiful hair on someone else is an act of your will. Not only does it bless the person who receives the compliment, it also leaves you open to fresh ideas about how to style your own hair.

Don't laugh at someone else's bad hair day. We all have bad hair days. We are all on this hair journey together. Some days you get it right and others don't. Sometimes they get it right and you don't. No matter the situation, to laugh at someone else's hair misfortune is to belittle yourself. To mock another person's hair is to throw mud at yourself. When someone is having a bad hair day, your encouragement helps them get up and go again. It gives them a chance to try again. It helps them to laugh again, hope again, try it again, and go at it again. Your encouragement helps someone else recover from discouragement. Your encouragement comes back to encourage you because it raises an army of people who will, in turn, come back to encourage you when it matters most.

Don't insist on your own way. Your hair is created with unique texture and consistency. She curls and kinks in particular ways. Allowing her to exist in her natural state helps her to thrive. Every time you insist on making her look a certain way that's different from her inner nature, you kill her natural creativity. Every time you ask her to be someone she is not, you encourage her to be ashamed. Don't do this to her. Instead, cater to her needs. Help her discover her natural beauty. Let her tell you how she likes to be styled. Define styles around what she likes best, not what you feel is most popular or culturally acceptable. Embrace her natural state: her coarseness, softness, and sponginess are all part of who she is. Accept her. Don't force her to go out of her way to please someone who doesn't even know, love, or understand her. Please love her for who she is.

Stay hopeful. As you go on your hair journey, you'll realize that there is so much about your hair that you don't know yet. Stay hopeful, for there is more to discover. Remember that you are on a journey of discovery. Stay optimistic that you will find your way. Know that what your hair looks like today is not what she will look like tomorrow. Tomorrow, with the right investment, the state of your hair can be better than it is today. If today seems discouraging, stay hopeful that tomorrow will be better. Because it will be.

Never give up. You will have bad hair days, hard hair days, terrible hair days, and crazy hair days. No matter the

7 Laws of black Hair

kind of hair day you're having, don't give up. If you'll just look up and catch a glimpse of the future, you will realize that there is a beautiful light at the end of the dark hair tunnel. At the beginning of your hair discovery, you may get discouraged. You will want to throw in the towel and forget all about your hair. You will wish you were born with a completely different texture. You may wish you were born a different race. You may even wish you were naturally bald! But take each day one step at a time. Smile big and try again. Endure the worst hair days because the next hair day will be better. Never lose faith. Never give up!

Benefits of Hair Love

As you practice the habits of hair love, your hair love will grow. Hair love takes time to develop. It takes time and investment. However, when you actively love her, your hair is transformed and starts to thrive. Imagine how your hair will respond to this new-found love. Love can turn the most boring wall flower into a fantastic beauty. The benefits of hair love are immense. A few benefits are outlined below:

Your hair will love you back. Until now, your hair may have felt like the ugly stepsister. Until now, she may not have received the kind of love you are about to shower on her. As you lavish her with love, you will notice a difference in her: She will start to love you back. All of a sudden, you will find that she is smiling more. She'll have a spring in her step. When you least expect it, she will be humming a tune. She will start to make you look good. Really good. She will introduce you to people you have never met. On account of your hair loving you back, you will start to make new friends. You'll get great compliments. Your hair will respond to your love and people will notice. It will suddenly get easier to style her. You'll love her more each day. And she too, will love you more.

Your hair will thrive. Actively loving your hair causes her to thrive. Have you noticed what happens to a plant when you take it out of a dark room, add water to it, and put it in the sunlight? All of a sudden, that droopy plant perks up. The brown leaves grow green again and the plant is reborn. That is exactly what will happen for your hair. Her droopy locks will blossom. She will stand tall. She will start to look different and act in a way you had not imagined possible. She will cry a lot less, laugh more often, and look more beautiful. She will start to draw attention to herself because she will become so beautiful, everyone will notice.

Your hair will grow. With thriving comes growth. As you show her love and nurture her, your hair will grow. Really grow. Your gentle care, kindness, and generosity will free her up to grow. She will start to grow in a way you didn't think was possible. You will see her attain new lengths; longer than you had ever dreamed possible. Loving your hair will cause her to grow thick, luxurious, gorgeous, and beautiful. Loving your hair will make her grow.

Your hair will become a source of joy. As your hair starts to thrive, you will start to enjoy her company more. You will marvel at the different things she can do. You will be amazed at how gorgeously she curls, how beautifully she locks, how marvelously she twists. You will get to a point that, whenever you catch a glimpse of her in the mirror, you will smile. She will bring so much joy that you will have a new sense of who you are. She will bring you such joy that people will take notice, pay attention. They'll ask if you're in love. They'll stop just to see you smile. Your hair will bring joy to your life in a way you never thought possible.

Your hair will become a source of blessing. As your hair brings joy to your life, she will also become a source of blessing to others. She will start to attract people to her beauty in such a way as to make them sit up and pay attention. People will see her and smile to themselves. She will be a source of encouragement to others. She will help people see possibilities. She will help people see what they too can do with their own hair. For people who are struggling on their hair journey, your beautiful hair will be a source of inspiration to give them the strength to keep going. Your hair will bless others and give them wings to fly. Your love for your hair will cause her to bless others.

Obey the Law of Love

The first Law of Love is the most important law that applies to your hair. Love is the foundation of all relationships. Without love, there can be no true connection. Love allows your relationship to move from mere transaction to true engagement. When it comes to your hair, hair love is, indeed, the fulfillment of the entire law. Every other Law of Hair is built on the fundamental foundation and truth of this one law. Don't move past this law to the next until you have started to actively love your hair. Allow me to borrow a leaf from the Bible:

And you shall love [your hair] with all your heart and with all your soul and with all your strength.[3]

Love your hair; for in loving her, you love the One who created her and, in loving her, you ultimately love yourself.

The Law of
Investment

Every Investment Brings a Return

The Law of Investment

The law of investment states that, every investment you make in your hair will yield a return.

Definitions

The Merriam-Webster Dictionary defines "investment" and "return" in ways that are relevant to our discussion as follows:

Investment[1]

1. The act of putting out money in order to gain a profit.

2. A sum of money invested.

3. A property in which money is invested.

Return[2]

1. To bring in (profit).

2. The value of or profit from such venture.

3. The profit from labor, investment, or business.

From the above definitions, we can reword the Law of Investment as follows:

When you put money into your hair and count your hair as a property in which money is invested, you will bring in profit from your labor and investment.

I Hated to Spend Money on my Hair

When we were growing up, my hair was always done by my sister. She loved to create new styles and I was her willing and very appreciative hair model. No matter what she did to my hair, I always looked fantastic. As a result of my steady diet of free and fantastic hair, no matter how far apart we lived, I would always travel to her location to get my hair done.

One day, she announced that she would no longer be doing my hair. It wasn't personal, she assured me. She was tired of doing hair and had decided to cut everybody off from her personal source of hair goodness. From now on, everyone, including me, would have to find their own way.

Wow! Her decision stung. Me? Her favorite second sister? She would never do my hair again? Ever? This terrible news was too much to bear. What was I to do with my hair? After a lifetime of free hairstyles, I was to start paying out of pocket to get my own hair done?

I respected her decision, reluctantly. She was, after all, a brand new mom. As a new mom, she had many demands on her time and it was selfish of me to ask her to continue to invest in my hair. It was time for me to take responsibility for my own hair. Surely, I could make it work.

I started looking into "professional" hairstylists. Boy, were they expensive! I would find myself looking through the price lists with eyebrows raised. "Braids cost how much? No way!" I decided that getting one's hair done by anyone other than one's sister was too pricey. I didn't have enough money to "splurge" on my hair. If I was a rich woman, sure. But I was a student with a negative net worth and I was not about to borrow more money just to get my hair done. I made a decision, I would do my own hair myself and when I couldn't, I would look around for the cheapest options available.

Needless to say, at that time in my life, my hair reflected my minimal investment. It didn't grow long, shed frequently, and, every 6 to 8 bad hair jobs or so, I lost some hairline. But what was I to do? I couldn't afford to do otherwise. Spending real money on my hair was just not an option.

Fast forward a few years, and I could finally afford to pay to see a "professional" hairstylist. The first day I met Mrs. T., she asked me, "what are your hair goals?" Hair goals? What were those? You mean people had hair goals? As a goal-oriented person who, every year, without fail, sets personal goals for every aspect of my life, I was disappointed at this oversight. Somehow, I had missed the life session where I should have been taught about setting hair goals. I thought about her question for a moment, then answered quickly, "My goal is for my hair to be healthy. I don't care as much about length (I honestly didn't think my hair could grow). I really care about my hair's health." She seemed satisfied with my answer. "Phew!" It was a close call (I hate to be caught not knowing the right answer). And, that day, she asked no more questions.

Her question stayed with me. Hair goals? Really? People have hair goals? By now, the seed was planted and I had unwittingly committed myself to achieving optimal hair health. To accomplish this goal, I would need a strategy. I would need a strategy that would take a measure of a financial investment. A financial investment I had avoided, until now.

Define Your Hair Goals

What are your hair goals? Yes, what hair goals have you set for yourself? If you have never set hair goals for yourself before today, think carefully about them now. If you have previously given hair goals some thought, that's wonderful. But if you haven't, then this moment represents an opportunity to reflect on your hair and what you really want her to become.

In setting hair goals, it is helpful to think about your hair length and volume, curl definition, hair strength, and scalp texture.

1. **Hair length.** How long would you like your hair to be? Now, think realistically. Unless your hair is straightened, it is unlikely to cascade down your back. If your hair is like most *black* hair, no matter how long it gets, in its natural state, it will grow upward and outward, away from the ground. So perhaps, rather than hair length, think about your desired hair height. Think carefully about length in a way that truly defines you. How long would you like your hair to be? Now, don't use someone else's hair length as a standard for yours. Think independently of what you think you can or want to achieve that really beautifies you personally and uniquely.

2. **Hair volume.** How full would you like your hair to be? Be careful here. When people think about hair fullness, they tend to default to a look that can only be achieved with hair extensions, weaves, or artificial hair insertions. Try not to think about these artificial measures of hair volume. Think about your own hair and its potential for fullness. To help get a sense of what has previously been possible, go back to your childhood

pictures. How big was your hair then? How big would you like your hair to be in future?

3. **Curl definition.** How would you like your curls to appear? Would you like them to be tightly coiled, loose, or wavy? Or do you want to wear your hair straight? Again, think carefully about the image that really defines you and not someone else. Rather than dwell on society's misguided notions, think about your true ideals. How would you like your curls to be defined?

4. **Hair strength.** How strong would you like your hair to be? Think about your hair texture as you run your hands through her strands. Does she feel pretty strong right now? Is she limp, weak, full of split ends, or is she strong and sound with ends intact? What is your vision for her strength? What will it take to help her be as strong as you desire? How long will it take to get her there? What will it cost you? How much strength would you like her to have?

5. **Scalp texture.** How would you like your scalp to feel as you run your hands over it? Why not run your hands over your scalp right now? How does it feel under your fingertips? What is its texture? How many bumps do you run into? Is there any tenderness? How does your scalp feel right now? How would you like your scalp to feel in the future?

The above hair goals are not exhaustive. But, they should be a good start for helping you to think about what you'd like your hair to become. Thinking about what you'd like your future hair to look like is an important step in helping you define and set your hair goals.

Knowing your hair goals empowers you to act. Your future

hair goals help define your current actions. Taking action today is the only way you guarantee your hair's future, tomorrow. To take action today is to acknowledge your personal responsibility in this process. To set goals without taking action is to daydream. Don't just daydream; use your dreams as the blueprint upon which you build and refine your hair goals. By defining your dreams and vision for your hair, you now have a chance to make your hair dream, or vision, a reality.

Define Your Investment

Your hair investment strategy, then, is simply the series of actions you take toward achieving your hair goals. The first steps toward making the right investments start from determining your goals. Once you decide what you want to achieve, you can now work backwards to figure out the cost of what it will take to get there. Defining your goals helps you understand exactly how much you will need to invest today to achieve tomorrow's goals.

Refine Your Investment Strategy

For better or for worse, you are already making hair investments. Your investments are evident in the food you eat, the fluids you drink, the kinds of hair products you use, and the styles you do. If you have not previously defined your hair goals, then all the investments you have made up to this point have been somewhat useless. None of these investments were made with your true goals in mind. Every investment that has been made without respecting your real goals is like having a volunteer army that does not follow orders but, instead, does what it wants. It's like having an investment strategy without teeth. Your investments may be working hard, but there is no real progress. To make progress is to advance towards your goals. And now that your goals are clearly defined, you can change your investment strategy to better align with your goals. You can begin to make the right investments that will help you reach your long-term goals.

Determine Your Investment Horizon

You cannot fully understand how much you need to invest until you clarify your investment horizon. Simply put, your investment horizon is the amount of time that you are willing to wait to achieve maximum returns.[3] As it applies to financial investments, it also applies to your hair: The longer your investment horizon, the better the returns you can expect to achieve. The longer your investment horizon, the less you have to put in every day to achieve your goals.

Investigate Before You Invest

Before you make any investment, you must exercise due diligence and investigate the investment. When it comes to hair investment products, there are so many to choose from. From the ones that will make your hair grow fast to the one that will make your hair grow long. Whatever the claim of the hair investment vehicle, you must investigate the investment to be sure that it suits the needs of your hair. You must check it out to confirm that it is a product that will not cost you more in the long run. Investigating the investment gives you both the understanding and confidence to invest. Investing with confidence sets you free from the peer pressure that drives many to invest in products they do not really understand.

Create a Unique Investment Portfolio

Create your own unique investment portfolio. Your hair is unique and so are you. When you acknowledge your uniqueness, then you recognize that what suits someone else does not fit you exactly. Your hair, her texture, her needs, and wants are unique to you. What makes someone else's hair thrive may not work for your hair. Therefore, don't just listen to the crowd. Determine what works best for your hair and make an informed decision so that you can create a hair investment portfolio that is uniquely tailored to you.

Start Investing Early

The earlier you start investing in your hair, the better your hair returns. The key to starting early is that you develop the good habits that will sustain your hair over a lifetime of healthy returns. Starting early also saves you more in the long term because, over several years of investment, less investment is needed to achieve the same returns.

To think of this in practical terms, the best time to start investing in your hair is during your childhood. When tender hairlines are protected and a young scalp is tenderly nourished, permanent hair damage and significant hair loss are avoided. If you did not have this same kind of hair investment in childhood and hair damage has already occurred, to reverse these negative effects, more costly investments are needed later in life.

An early investment strategy is best achieved with the help of mothers, fathers, and caregivers of young children. Helping young children to start their hair investment early makes a significant impact on their hair future. Their hair future is secured through intentional investments that bring maximum lifetime hair returns.

Invest Regularly and Consistently

Your investments go further when you invest regularly and consistently. This kind of consistent investment is similar to what is known in financial terms as dollar cost averaging.[4] Investing every day gets you used to investing and helps to automate your actions. Investing a little each day yields more returns than a big, lavish, one-time investment. The sacrifice of daily investing, no matter the cost, is what your hair really needs.

Seek Long-Term Gains

To achieve your hair goals is a lifetime endeavor. Your head of hair was with you at birth and will be with you at death. Therefore, every investment you make in your hair must take the long-term, lifelong view into perspective. Don't fall for "grow-hair-quick" schemes that promise you short-term gains but, in the long term, hurt your hair. Every investment that promises quick returns is likely to cost you more in the end. Think long term. The best investors are in it for the long haul. Take your time and invest in your hair wisely.

Diversify Your Portfolio

Every successful investor must have a diversified portfolio. Your hair is dynamic and will be there with you through the different phases of your life. She will stick with you through the ups and downs and joys and successes of life. It's OK to try out different styles, test novel products, seek out a new hairstylist, cut your hair off, or grow her really long. Doing new things refreshes your hair and, in turn, refreshes your life. Your hair is energetic, spirited, and active and she craves adventure as much (or as little) as you do. She craves variety and you should diversify your hair portfolio to bring out the very best in her.

The strength of a diversified hair portfolio can be understood by examining the individual components of a good hair portfolio. A few resources that make up a well-diversified investment portfolio are outlined below:

1. **Money.** Money is the primary hair investment medium. You will likely use money to buy hair products, pay a hairstylist, finance hair treatments, and buy foods that improve your hair health. However, while money is very important, and will factor into how and what you invest, it is not the only investment tool at your disposal.

2. **Food.** When it comes to your hair, food is probably your most important investment vehicle. Maintaining a balanced diet that is full of all the nutrients necessary for a healthy body is also essential to maintaining hair health. Fad diets that result in significant caloric restriction and starve you of essential nutrients are damaging to your hair health. A good food investment portfolio ensures a diet rich in fruits, vegetables, lean protein, and whole grains.[5]

3. **Water.** A most essential nutrient, water is an essential part of a diversified hair investment portfolio. Water is the fluid of our lives. Water helps maintain the balance of body fluids involved in transporting vital nutrients to your hair.[6] Your hair needs to stay hydrated because she thrives in an atmosphere of moisture. In Chapter 5, the Law of Moisture, you will learn more about the importance of moisture to your hair.

4. **Hair products.** Second only to the money spent buying food, most of the money invested in our hair will be spent buying hair products. When it comes to hair products, please choose carefully. With so many available hair products whose claims I have not tested, it would be unwise for me to attempt to review them in this book. I will, however, mention that you should avoid hair products that dry out your hair and prioritize

those that promote moisture and help add crucial oils.

5. **Hairstylists.** Hairstylists are a vital part of your
   investment portfolio. If you do not pay a professional
   hairstylist, you likely get your hair done by your mother,
   a sister, aunt, grandma, or friend. For the purposes of
   your hair investment portfolio, a hairstylist is someone
   other than you who does your hair. Therefore, with so
   many "kitchen" stylists to choose from, choose your
   hairstylist wisely. Make sure that she is as interested in
   your hair health as she is in helping you look good. A
   hairstylist who will refuse to do a style because of the
   damage it may cause to your hair is worth her weight in
   gold.

6. **Hairstyles.** Not every hairstyle is a worthy investment.
   All hairstyles are not created equal. Some hairstyles
   add to the health of your hair while others devalue
   her. Some hairstyles protect your hair while others
   damage it. Sometimes, a hairstyle looks good but will
   temporarily or permanently cause damage to your hair.
   Weigh every hairstyle carefully to understand whether
   it is worth the investment. A poorly chosen hairstyle
   can undo years of sound hair investment. Choose your
   hairstyle investment portfolio judiciously. A diversified
   hair investment portfolio makes use of the resources
   you have available to create the best hair investment
   package that fulfills your goals.

Expect a Return on Your Investment

Every investment you make in your hair will yield a
return. For better or for worse, some of the returns you
are experiencing today come from the good and bad
investments you made several years ago. Now that you have
read this chapter on the Law of Investment, you have a

chance to make a different choice.

Your job is to ensure that your investment portfolio lines up with the goals you have outlined for your hair. As soon as you determine that your investments and goals align, then pour as much energy as you can into maximizing your investments. Without a targeted investment strategy, the returns you seek will never come. The more strategically you invest, the more of your clearly defined and anticipated returns you can expect to see. The longer your investment horizon, the better your returns. The earlier you start investing, the more returns you can expect to see over time. Do everything you can to make the right investments in your hair today.

The Law of Retention

You Keep What You Retain

The Law of Retention

The Law of Retention states that the key to hair growth is retention.

Definitions

The Merriam-Webster Dictionary defines "grow" and "retain" in ways that are relevant to our discussion as follows:

Grow[1]

1. To increase in size.

2. To spring up and develop to maturity.

3. To become increasingly acceptable or attractive.

Retain[2]

1. To keep in possession or use.

2. To keep in one's pay or service.

3. To hold secure or intact.

From the above definitions, we can reword the Law of Retention as follows:

The key to your hair increasing in size, springing up, developing to maturity, and becoming increasingly acceptable or attractive, is to keep her in possession or use, keep her in your pay or service, and hold her secure and intact.

My Hair Would not Grow

Until I was in my 30s, my hair did not grow past a certain length. It appeared that, no matter what I did, my hair was destined to get to a certain length and stop growing. I once discussed this problem with a stylist and she told me that it was likely a genetic problem. Perhaps, in my family, she explained, hair did not grow past a certain length. I thought about her explanation and felt that it was quite a good one. My mother's hair had never grown that long and neither had her mother's hair before her. How could one argue with genetics? If my genes determined how long my hair could grow, then who was I to argue or complain.

I was satisfied with the "genetics" explanation until my daughter was born. Over the first few years of her life, I watched her hair grow until it was almost double the length of my own. I wondered, "How could this child," then 3 years old, "have hair that was longer than mine? How did the genes that presumably controlled my own hair growth somehow bypass her?" For the first time, my assumptions regarding the capacity for my hair growth were challenged. I became determined that, if my daughter's hair could grow long, then so could mine.

I set a goal for hair growth and started working towards it. Much to my surprise, I found that my hair could grow too! Wow! After over 30 years of living on the earth, it took my 3-year old daughter to challenge my deeply held assumptions about what kind of hair length it was possible for me to achieve. Knowing what was possible set me free to take the steps necessary to make my hair length goals a reality. The genetic "lie" would no longer hold me back.

The Biology of Hair Growth

Every hair strand begins in a small structure called a hair follicle.[3] Up to 150,000 hair follicles come together to make a full head of hair. Each follicle independently goes through a unique cycle that is characterized by phases of growth, transformation, and rest.[4] At any given time, about 90% of the hair follicles on your scalp are in a growth phase. During this phase, the average hair strand will grow at a rate of approximately 0.3 mm a day. At 0.3 mm of daily growth, each hair strand will grow about 4 inches a year (0.3 mm a day converted to inches and multiplied by 365 days a year). This growth phase can last anywhere from 2 to 8 years. Following the growth period, the hair follicle enters into a state of transformation where hair production stops. Once hair production stops, the follicle enters into rest. During the rest phase, the hair falls out. Up to 150 hair strands fall out each day. At any given time, about 10% of hair follicles are in this state of rest. At the end of rest, the follicle enters into the growth phase and the cycle begins anew.

Hair Growth Depends on Many Factors

Hair growth depends on many factors, such as your diet, environment, the health of your scalp, and, yes, genetics. The factors that affect hair growth tend to directly or indirectly impact the hair follicle cycle described above. How long each hair follicle stays in its growth phase can determine hair length. However, hair length can just as easily be affected by premature entry into or prolonged stay in the transformation and rest phases. For instance, factors that can cause hair follicles to enter into the transformation and rest phase and result in excessive hair shedding, include the effect of medications, illness, iron deficiency, stress, and malnutrition. Sometimes, the inciting problem will not cause hair loss until 2 to 4 months later. When hair loss does occur, it can last for several months. Assuming the underlying problem is corrected, and permanent damage has not occurred, once hair loss abates, the hair follicle will again enter into the growth stage and the cycle will begin all over again.

Your Hair Can and Does Grow

All hair, including *black* hair, grows. This constant cycle of growth, transformation, and rest applies to all hair types. However, when compared to other hair types, *black* hair tends to grow a little slower. On average, *black* hair grows at a rate of 0.265 mm a day, which translates to about 3.8 inches a year.[5] Note that these numbers only represent statistical averages and likely do not reflect your own personal hair growth rate. Your hair growth rate is likely well known to you. You may not be able to state your exact growth rate in millimeters or inches; but you can usually gauge your hair growth based on how long it takes until a style you are wearing starts to look messy. You can tell your hair growth rate based on how long it takes your dyed roots to show or how long it takes before hair "undergrowth" needs attention. Each person has a sense of exactly how fast their hair tends to grow, and you should be familiar with yours.

The Problem is not Growth, but Retention

Hair growth is typically not the problem; rather, retention is. Retaining the hair you grow is the single most important factor in achieving maximum hair length. If you struggle with hair growth, look for potential underlying causes that may affect your retention. Some important hair retention factors that may undermine your hair growth and contribute to hair loss are the following:

1. **Poor diet.** Some diets that severely restrict calories and/or protein intake can lead to non-permanent hair loss. Hair regrowth can be promoted by getting back on a balanced diet and maximizing your nutrition.

2. **Medication.** Certain medications contribute to reversible hair loss.[6] If you are on any medications that you think may be contributing to hair loss, review the list with the prescribing health care provider. Together, you can discuss your concerns and talk about what changes can be made.

3. **Iron deficiency.** Iron deficiency affects many women who have monthly menstrual periods. Iron deficiency can be associated with significant hair loss.[7] A simple test administered by your health care provider can check for iron deficiency. If present, iron deficiency can be easily treated.

4. **Stress.** A common cause of reversible hair loss is stress.[8] Getting rid of stress can be difficult but is an important part of avoiding hair loss. Stress avoidance is hard. Rather than try unsuccessfully to passively avoid stress, try to actively pursue things that bring peace instead. Systematically pursuing a peaceful state is one way to contribute toward both your overall health and hair retention.

A Word About Split Ends

A discussion about hair retention would not be complete without addressing split ends. Split ends are damaged strands of hair, which tend to occur toward the end of the hair strand and split the hair shaft down its length.[9] Split ends occur as a result of mechanical, chemical, or thermal stress. They can be caused by vigorous brushing, chemical treatments, excessive heat, and hair dyes. Split ends can further be exacerbated by hair that is dry and brittle.

The best way to prevent split ends is by taking great care of your hair. Treating your locks tenderly helps to minimize damage to the hair shaft. Harsh treatments that can compromise your hair's structural integrity are best avoided. If, despite good preventative strategies, split ends occur, the best way to avoid their extension down the hair shaft is to cut them off. A periodic trim, occurring every few months, can help to minimize the damage that can be caused by having split ends.

Damaged Hair Can Grow Again

Many hair growth or length retention disorders are reversible. As long as there has not been permanent loss of hair follicles, the hair follicle stands a chance of re-entering the growth phase. For instance, nutritional deficiencies can be addressed; styles that lead to prolonged tension on the hair follicle can be avoided; and infections affecting hair growth can be treated.[10] The most important step in recovering lost hair is intentionality. Be intentional about recovering the hair you seek to regain. Remain hopeful and set new goals. Once you have set new goals, start investing intentionally with tenacity. If you desire to regain lost length, sincerely work at it. Your hair can and will grow back. Indeed, all things, including hair recovery, are possible to the woman who believes.[11]

If Your Hair is Damaged, Reach Out for Help

If you struggle with hair growth, retention, or loss, please reach out for help. Find a hair doctor who can assess your hair situation and give you strategies for healing.

Sometimes, the decisions you made early in life, before you had a full understanding of how they would affect your hair, resulted in significant damage to your hair growth capacity. This realization can contribute to guilt and an unwillingness to seek help. Don't let past mistakes keep you from getting the help that you need. As with all problems affecting the human body, healing will likely take time; but the possibility of restoration to optimal hair health is always worth the pursuit.

The Law of Moisture

What is Brittle Will Break

The Law of Moisture

The Law of Moisture states that when moisture is added to your hair, it prevents brittleness.

Definitions

The Merriam-Webster Dictionary defines "moisture" and "brittle" in ways that are relevant to our discussion as follows:

Moisture[1]

1. Liquid diffused or condensed in relatively small quantity.

2. A small amount of liquid that makes something wet or moist.

3. A small amount of liquid that causes moistness.

Brittle[2]

1. Easily broken, cracked, or snapped.

2. Easily disrupted, overthrown, or damaged.

3. Easily hurt or offended

From the above definitions, the Law of Moisture can be reworded as follows:

When a small amount of liquid is added to your hair to make it wet or moist, it prevents your hair from becoming easily broken, cracked, snapped, disrupted, overthrown, damaged, hurt, or offended.

My Hair was Brittle

When I learned how to do my own two-strand twists, they became my go-to hairstyle. They were easy to put in and easy to take out. I loved them and I wore them every day. Two-strand twists were awesome.

At the same time that I stumbled-upon two-strand twists, I also discovered the amazing power of hair gel. Hair gel, I thought, was a gift from heaven. Hair gel was easy to find and provided maximum hold for the styles I desired. I heavily patronized hair gel, buying the cheapest brands I could find and using the maximum amount possible. Hair gel was awesome!

Not so awesome, however, was the damage it was doing to my hair. For some "strange" reason, a few months after I began using hair gel, each time I combed or brushed out my hair, I found short hair strands everywhere. Everywhere I looked, I was losing massive amounts of hair. My hair was suffering significant breakage. Unfortunately, I was young, naïve, and uninformed and couldn't put the two – excessive hair gel and hair breakage – together. I knew something was wrong; but I wasn't sure how to fix it.

I finally went to see a hairstylist. After just a few minutes of brushing my hair, she exclaimed in horror, "What is going on with your hair?" She was dismayed at the sad state of my brittle, fragile, and breakable hair. I sat in her stylist's chair, sheepish, embarrassed, and apologetic. I sat there quietly, not knowing exactly what to say. She was appalled, and I was ashamed. I was ashamed because I could have and should have known better, but didn't. I couldn't have known that the hair gel could wreak such havoc on my hair. Or could I?

black Hair is Fragile Hair

Of the three distinct hair types in the world – African (or *black*), Asian, and Caucasian – *black* hair is the most fragile. Not only is *black* hair the most fragile, she is also the most susceptible to breakage.[3] Although all three hair types have the exact same protein composition, *black* hair differs in her mechanical properties, tensile strength, and water absorption.

1. ***black* hair absorbs the least water.** When it comes to water absorption, among the 3 hair types, *black* hair absorbs the least amount of water. She absorbs the least amount of water and, thus, compared to other hair types, needs more hydration.

2. ***black* hair breaks more easily under lower stress conditions.** When uniform amounts of stress are applied to each hair type, *black* hair breaks more easily under lower stress conditions. When compared to other hair types, *black* hair is both more fragile and breaks more easily. Compared to other hair types, *black* hair needs to be handled more carefully.

3. ***black* hair has a unique shape.** Another explanation for *black* hair's fragility comes from its shape. In contrast to other hair types, which have straight hair follicles and round hair shafts with homogeneous diameters and no irregularities, *black* hair has an elliptical shape with flattened and irregular hair shafts.[4] This property gives *black* hair lower tensile strength and resistance and increases her susceptibility to breakage. Additionally, the irregularities in shape contribute to *black* hair's tendency towards forming knots and tangles, easily. Therefore, compared to other hair types, *black* hair's unique shape needs more careful

attention.

4. ***black hair* needs more oils.** Although all hair
types tend to produce the same amount of natural hair
oils, *black* hair needs extra oils. *black* hair needs extra
oils because of the unique angle at which the strand
emerges from the hair follicle. Compared to Asian and
Caucasian hair types, *black* hair emerges from the follicle
almost parallel to the scalp. This parallel emergence,
combined with the coiled pattern of the hair shaft,
prevents natural hair oils, sebum, from distributing all
along the hair shaft. The uneven distribution of sebum
along the hair shaft accounts for the lack of sheen that
characterizes *black* hair. Therefore, *black* hair needs the
addition of extra hair oils.

black Hair Needs Tender Loving Care

From the above, you may now understand that *black* hair's
unique properties make her very susceptible to drying out
and becoming brittle. When you also consider that *black*
hair gets very easily tangled and frequently ends up in
knots, *black* hair desperately needs tender loving care. Due
to her exceptional nature, *black* hair should be handled
with a gentle touch, brushed with a loving hand, hydrated
extensively, and oiled regularly.

Your *black* Hair Needs Moisture

Your *black* hair has a tendency toward dryness and
brittleness. If you do nothing to your hair, and leave her
to her own devices, she will dry up, become brittle, break
easily, and suffer. Therefore, to leave your hair as she
is without addressing her basic need for moisture is to
overlook her needs. To meet your hair's needs, you should
actively work to overcome her natural tendencies towards

dryness and breakage.

To meet your hair's basic needs, it is important that you hydrate her, add essential oils to lock in moisture, and repeat the process again and again. Remember that your hair tends towards dryness so you will need to work actively to help her stay refreshed and moisturized.

The power to release your hair into a state of refreshing moisture, sheen, and glory, is in your hands. Will you break the cycle of brittleness over your hair and accept the challenge to obey the Law of Moisture. Obey the Law of Moisture and watch your hair thrive.

The Law of Protection

Weaknesses are to be Protected

The Law of Protection

The Law of Protection states that your hair's weaknesses are to be protected.

Definitions

The Merriam-Webster Dictionary defines "weak" and "protect" in ways that are relevant to our discussion as follows:

Weak[1]

1. Deficient in physical vigor.
2. Not able to sustain or exert much weight, pressure, or strain.
3. Not able to resist external force or withstand attack.

Protect[2]

1. To cover or shield from exposure, injury, damage, or destruction.
2. To defend.
3. To maintain the status or integrity of.

Therefore, from the above definitions, the Law of Protection can be reworded as follows:

Your hair is deficient in physical vigor; not able to sustain or exert much weight, pressure, or strain; and not able to resist external force or withstand attack. Therefore, in order to maintain her status and integrity, she is to be defended and shielded from exposure, injury, damage, and destruction.

Our Hairline was Under Attack

In my family, the women are born with very fine hair. The hair around our hairlines, in particular, is very delicate and breaks easily. When we were children, my sisters and I would often go to the hairstylist to get our hair braided. In an attempt to keep the styles neat for long periods of time, the braids were pulled quite tight. As they pulled at our hairlines, these tight styles were a major source of tears. But more important than the tears we shed was the contribution of these tight styles to hair loss. Unfortunately, over time, these tight styles prevailed, and our hairlines lost ground.

One day, my younger sister returned from a visit to our hometown. She came back with big news – our hair loss was hereditary! Apparently, every woman in the entire town had receding hairlines. Our hairlines were doomed by our ancestors and there was nothing we could do about it. We held no hope of ever recovering hairline growth. What terrible news. How awful it was for us to discover that our hairlines were forever doomed to recede. How dreadful to know that we were destined to pass on this heritable hair loss to our daughters. Or were we?

black Hair Does not Tolerate Stress Well

In the preceding chapter, the Law of Moisture, I explain the unique properties of *black* hair that increase her tendency towards fragility. To recap, when compared to other hair types, *black* hair absorbs less water, breaks more easily, has less oil sheen, and tangles more frequently. Due to her natural configuration, *black* hair needs more hydration, more oils added, and more careful handling.

It is pertinent to note that, in her natural state, before any physical, chemical, or thermal manipulation is applied, *black* hair requires handling with great care. Once any manipulation is applied to *black* hair, even more careful attention is needed. Therefore, *black* hair that is not specially cared for will show signs of neglect.

Neglected *black* Hair is Easily Damaged

Neglected *black* hair is *black* hair that has been subjected to mechanical, chemical, or thermal treatment without regard to her basic needs and stress tolerance. If, based on her unique structure, *black* hair needs hydration, extra oils, and extreme care, then any treatment that blatantly ignores these needs is, at best, negligent or, at worst, downright abusive.

Neglectful or abusive hair practices ignore the peculiar needs of *black* hair and exploit her weaknesses, leading to the increased likelihood of irreparable damage. Repeated instances of damage to the *black* hair structure can result in uncontrolled hair loss. Premature and/or excessive hair loss can undermine your hair's desire to be seen in public and present a challenge to your self esteem.

Ignoring the weaknesses of your *black* hair can undermine her strength. Systematically undermining her strength can lead to a number of hair disorders. The hair disorders that affect *black* hair are many; but I have outlined 3 common and potentially preventable disorders below:

Hair breakage.[3] As implied by its name, hair breakage is a syndrome that is characterized by excessive hair loss due to fragility. When hair breakage is present, your hair is affected by simple everyday actions. Actions such as brushing your hair or resting your head on a pillow can result in breakage of the hair shaft at its point of exit from the scalp.

Some people are born with hair breakage syndrome but, for most people, it is an acquired problem. Acquired causes of hair breakage include long-term use of chemical straighteners, continuous use of heat styling, and excessive combing or brushing with stiff combs. If hair breakage syndrome is recognized early, prompt treatment can be applied to decrease the possibility of unrecoverable hair loss due to permanent scarring. Avoidance of permanent scarring increases the probability of future hair regrowth.

Traction Alopecia.[4] Defined simply, traction alopecia is hair loss that occurs when hair is forcefully pulled out of the hair follicle. One of the most common disorders affecting *black* hair, traction hair loss is characterized by shortening of the hairs in the front of the scalp at the place where the hairline starts. Signs of traction hair loss include redness around the front hairline. A common sight is the presence of hair strands with a white substance on the end. The white substance on the end of the hair strands signifies that hair was pulled directly out of the follicle.

Traction hair loss is frequently caused by firm hairstyles, tight ponytails, and heavy hairpieces that apply prolonged pressure to the hairline. If repeated episodes of traction cause continued prolonged pressure, the hairline recedes and hair follicles can be permanently lost. If traction hair loss is discovered early and the underlying cause addressed, lost hairline can still be recovered. Nevertheless, the primary way to avoid traction hair loss is prevention.

Central Centrifugal Cicatricial Alopecia (CCCA).[5] CCCA defines a group of hair disorders where permanent

7 Laws of black Hair

hair loss starts in the middle of the scalp and spreads outwards. In this disorder, hair follicles are replaced with scar tissue, leading to permanent hair loss. The direct causes of CCCA are not known; however, predisposing factors are thought to include genetic inheritance, hair-straightening chemicals, some heat-styling techniques, and hairstyles that pull excessively.

As mentioned earlier, the above 3 are just the "tip of the iceberg" of hair disorders that can affect *black* hair. Nevertheless, they highlight the prevalence of hair loss disorders that can be prevented.

Prevent Hair Loss Disorders

Many common hair loss disorders can be prevented. The subject of hair loss prevention is sensitive because it strikes at the heart of cultural and social norms surrounding *black* hairstyling practices. All hairstyling practices can and do contribute to hair loss. Therefore, the particular hairstyle is not so much the problem as is the sensitivity of the hair to the hairstyle. In other words, one *black* head of hair may thrive with a certain set of hairstyles where another many not. The key then, is not to avoid certain hairstyles altogether, but to find the right combination of hairstyles that bring out the best in **your** *black* hair.

Let's examine the pros and cons of a few common hairstyling practices.[6]

Natural hairstyles. For the purposes of this discussion, a "natural" hairstyle is defined as *black* hair that is styled without chemical or thermal alteration. Natural hairstyles are presumed to be the most protective. However, their ability to protect *black* hair from damage depends on how well they are managed. Some examples of natural hairstyles are as follows:

1. **Natural hair worn loose**. Probably the most economical hairstyle, natural *black* hair worn loose is typically called an "Afro" or 'fro. The benefits of the 'fro include ease of styling and avoidance of heat and chemical treatment-induced hair damage. Damage, however, can result from constant hair exposure to the elements (wind and sun), which can lead to excessive dryness and breakage. Additionally, frequent brushing and/or combing can lead to mechanical trauma. To maintain a healthy 'fro, careful attention should be paid to moisturizing the hair regularly and incorporating styles that protect the hair ends.

2. **Natural hair worn in a ponytail.** Another economical style, natural hair worn in a ponytail is second only to the 'fro because an investment must be made in a hair band or scrunchie. Wearing natural hair in a ponytail is easy and requires no forethought. However, if worn too tight, a ponytail can pull at the hairline and contribute to traction hair loss. Even when not worn tight, several years of a ponytail-only hairstyle can contribute to hairline loss. Additionally, excessive brushing can contribute to mechanical trauma. For best results, other hairstyles should be incorporated.

3. **Natural hair worn in a protective style.** Protective styles include twists and cornrows. These styles protect the hair from the elements and help to reduce split ends. If done too tight, however, they can contribute to traction hair loss. If left in too long, they cause the hair to form knots that, if not carefully undone, can contribute to mechanical trauma. For best results,

protective styles should be taken out and refreshed regularly.

4. **Natural hair worn in locs.** Hair locs combine several strands of hair to form a single unit, until the parent hair strands are indistinguishable from one another. Locs protect the hair ends and minimize the natural fallout that occurs during the hair follicle's rest phase. Locs, however, are still susceptible to hair breakage and can also cause traction hair loss. For best results, locs should be carefully moisturized and new hair growth should be regularly incorporated into existing locs.

Heat styling. Heat-based straightening styles can be achieved with the use of appliances such as hair dryers, hot combs, and flat irons. These tools produce heat that dehydrates the hair and causes temporary breakage of the bonds between the hair filaments. Breakage of these hair filament bonds causes the hair to straighten. The straightening caused by heat styling is typically reversed by the addition of moisture. However, if too high temperatures are reached, holes can form in the hair shaft, thereby increasing susceptibility to breakage.

1. **Occasional heat styling.** Typically, when done infrequently, the hair straightening achieved by heat styling is reversible. The bonds between the hair filaments, which were temporarily broken, can be reversed by the addition of moisture. If excessive heat is applied, however, irreversible damage to the hair shaft may occur. Care must also be taken to avoid thermal burns to the surrounding scalp, ears, and neck.

2. **Frequent heat styling.** Over time, regular heat styling can result in a semi-permanent hair

straightening where the hair does not return to its pre-heat-styled state. This state can be brought on by the gradual thinning of the outer layers of the hair, which becomes more fragile and susceptible to breakage.

For best results, heat styling should be used infrequently and, when done, excessive heat should be avoided.

Chemical straightening. Chemical straightening involves the use of chemicals to irreversibly disrupt the bonds between the hair filaments, resulting in permanently straightened hair. Chemical straightening can involve the use of a "relaxer" to obtain very straight hair or the use of a "texturizer" to maintain a looser version of the recipient's original curl pattern.

1. **Hair relaxers.** Hair relaxers typically come in two flavors: Lye and no-lye relaxers. Their active ingredients include sodium hydroxide (lye) and calcium hydroxide or guanidine hydroxide (no-lye). When applied to hair, these chemicals irreversibly break bonds between hair filaments and result in permanent straightening. When compared to chemically-untreated hair, relaxed hair is free of knots and more manageable. However, the chemicals in a relaxer are toxic and can cause chemical burns, damage the hair shaft, inflame the scalp, and increase hair fragility. Long-term application of relaxers can cause thinning of the hair and permanent hair loss.[7] For best results, seek the assistance of a professional, and limit application of chemical straighteners to new growth only.

2. **Texturizers.** Like relaxers, texturizers contain sodium hydroxide and calcium hydroxide as active ingredients. Some no-lye texturizers contain ammonium thioglycolate. Texturizers work similarly to relaxers but,

7 Laws of black Hair

rather than straighten the hair, the end result is loose curls. Texturizers and hair relaxers are essentially the same thing with hair texturizers achieving their curly effect by being left in the hair for a shorter period of time. The same side effects of hair relaxers apply to texturizers.

Hair extensions. Hair extensions can be applied to *black* hair in the form of braids, weaves, hair pieces, and wigs. Hair extensions are popular because they can be used to achieve different hair lengths and volume. Extension-based hairstyles are typically left in for periods of weeks to months and can be protective. Though uncommon, allergic reactions to synthetic hair have been reported.

1. **Hair braids.** Hair braids are extensions that can be incorporated into individual hair sections, braided into cornrows, or attached directly to the hair. Braids can be worn as protective styles because they shelter the hair shaft from the natural elements for extended periods of time. However, braids that are done too tightly or that are heavier than the strands of hair to which they are attached, can pull on the hair and cause traction hair loss. Traction hair loss can also occur when braids have been left in for prolonged periods of time. For best results, braids should be carefully done so as not to exert significant pull on the hairline and they should be taken out and replaced regularly.

2. **Hair pieces.** Hair pieces are human or synthetic hair pieces that are attached to the existing hair by means of clips, bobby pins, combs, thread, or glue. Hair pieces enable style versatility and can add volume to hair. However, when hair pieces are heavier than the hair to which they are attached, traction hair loss can occur.

3. **Hair weaves.** As with braids, weaves can help shelter the hair from the elements and are used for protective styling. Depending on how they attach to the hair, they can cause some pull on the hairline. Over time, they also can lead to traction-related hair loss. For best results, weaves should be inserted carefully to minimize hairline damage. They should also be removed and refreshed regularly to minimize their pull on the underlying hair.

4. **Wigs**. Wigs are hair extensions that are made to be worn over the scalp and hair. Wigs are easy to wear and do not tend to cause significant damage to the underlying hair. They are beneficial in that they can help to cover up temporary or permanent damage to the underlying hair. However, wigs can damage the hairline and hinder hair growth. Another disadvantage of wigs is that, by hiding her from view, they overshadow the glory of *black* hair. For best results, wigs should be worn temporarily and alternated with other styles that allow the underlying hair to breathe.

Choose styles that help your hair thrive. You may notice that the above list is not a comprehensive list of all possible *black* hairstyles. Nevertheless, the hairstyles above are highlighted to make the point that, if *black* hair is not properly cared for, any hairstyle can be damaging. Some hairstyles result in more consistent damage than others; however, careful study of your individual hair type is needed to determine which styles cause greater damage and which ones allow your *black* hair to thrive.

Your hair thrives under different circumstances than the hair belonging to your friends and loved ones. Therefore, rather than follow the crowd, take time to understand your hair type and the factors that help her thrive. Choosing hairstyles that help your hair thrive and avoiding those that undermine her health are critical to your hair's wellbeing. Make informed decisions about your hairstyle choices. Yes, the choice is always yours; but please choose wisely. Choose wisely and pay attention to your hair's weaknesses.

Weaknesses are to be Protected

When you discover that someone you love dearly has significant weaknesses, the correct response is one of protection. As the Law of Protection reveals, weaknesses are to be defended and shielded from exposure, injury, damage, and destruction. The responsibility for protecting your hair is yours. No one will protect her like you can. To protect her is to fulfill the Law of Love. To protect her is to put her needs and priorities above the whims of everyone else around you. To protect her is to let go of cultural norms and traditions to help your hair be her best self. To protect your hair is to protect your own interests because, in protecting her, you protect yourself.

Here are a few ways in which you can protect your hair:

1. **Protect your hair from pain.** When it comes to your hair, do not accept pain as part of your experience. I repeat, do not accept pain. When I was young and uninformed, I thought hairstyling was synonymous with pain. Now I understand that getting your hair done should never hurt. If it hurts your hair, note the person who inflicts the pain and don't ever go back. It doesn't matter if it was cheap, or even free. Never go back to any hairstylist, friend or foe, who has inflicted pain.

2. **Protect your hair from breakage.** Breakage is

not an inevitable fact of *black* hair. Condition your hair and provide the maximum support of essential oils (not petroleum jelly). Dry and brittle hair breaks easily but flexible and pliable hair bends effortlessly and proves hard to break.

3. **Protect your hair from loss.** There are so many styles you can do. Many of them were handed down from generations of your ancestors. Many of them are popular hairstyles done by people around you. Do me a favor, if it causes hair loss, let go of your preconceived notions and desire to please people and do the right thing. Unless the people around you, who are telling you what to do with your hair, will cut their own hair into a wig for you to wear once all your hair is gone, get smart! Protect your hair from loss.

4. **Protect your hair for the future.** While you're young and beautiful, your hair is more forgiving and can tolerate the worst kinds of stress. But, as you get older, the choices you make today will become more obvious in the integrity of your hairline. Consider whether your future hair will approve of the choices you make now. If there is any question that she would frown upon any decision you make today, stop! Turn around and let go of your bad choices. Make the right decisions that allow you to be beautiful both today and in the future. Protect your future hair.

5. **Protect your children's hair.** As a parent, grandparent, or relative, you hold the health and hair-esteem of your children in your hands. Use this great power wisely. Help them avoid styles that undermine the integrity of their future hairlines. Help them speak language that reflects the beauty and the glory of their

hair. Help them see how beautiful *black* hair is and can be. Please, for the sake of their future, protect your children's hair.

6. **Protect your hair from the ignorant.** Anyone who is not educated about *black* hair, including uneducated people with *black* hair, should not be dispensing advice that undermines the glory of your hair. If it sounds like it's bad advice, table it and go get more information. Don't allow ignorance to cost you your hair beauty.

7. **Protect your hair from people who hate her.** For whatever reason, some people actually hate *black* hair. I'm not sure why and I don't know how to begin to explain it; but do me a favor and avoid hatred in any form that it comes to your hair. Whether it be name-calling, eye-rolling, hair-pulling, or any kind of damage. Whatever the form of hair abuse, don't tolerate it. Run in the other direction. Run like the wind!

If you don't protect your hair, and by association, yourself, over time, you will suffer irreparable hair loss and permanently alter your hair beauty forever. When it comes to your hair weaknesses, it is time to take a stand. Whose honor will you defend? Your hair's or the status quo? The choice is yours today.

The Law of Investigation

What is not Investigated is Misunderstood

The Law of Investigation
The Law of Investigation states that hair that is not investigated is misunderstood.

Definitions
The Merriam-Webster Dictionary defines "investigate" and "understand" in ways that are relevant to our discussion as follows:

Investigate[1]
1. To observe by close examination and systematic inquiry.
2. To make a systematic examination.
3. To conduct an official inquiry.

Understand[2]
1. To grasp the meaning of.
2. To grasp the reasonableness of.
3. To be thoroughly familiar with the character and propensities of.

Based on the above definitions, the Law of Investigation can be reworded as follows:

One cannot grasp the meaning or reasonableness of, or be thoroughly familiar with the character and propensities of hair that has not been observed by close examination or systematic inquiry.

My Hair is Fine

"Your hair is very fine," the hairstylist remarked, "but you have high hair density." By now, that comment was a familiar one. Each time a new hairstylist examined my hair, the observation was repeated – I had very fine hair with a high concentration of hair follicles. The observation surprised each commentator because my hair's full appearance did not match what they expected when they examined the diameter of my hair fibers.

My hair fibers define my fine hair. The diameter of each hair fiber is small, which makes my hair appear fluffy. In Chapter 2, the Law of Love, I describe my experience with getting my hair straightened. With heat straightening, my fine hair fibers struggled to hold their own against the wind. It was not just the strong Chicago wind, but also the characteristic response of my hair. When straightened, my fine hair fibers become separated from each other and are no longer held together by my usually tangled coils. Untangled from her community of coils, each wispy strand must stand on her own to defend herself against the elements. The result is that my hair hangs limp against my face and any little breeze blows it all over the place.

Fortunately, because I have a good understanding of the properties of my own hair, I adjust my styling expectations to match what suits her best. Knowing her idiosyncrasies helps me make informed decisions about how I style my hair. Because my fine hair is extra fragile, I routinely choose hairstyles that incorporate my fine strands into a stronger braid or twist. I also tend to pursue styles with defined curls because they give my hair more volume. Knowing intimate details about my hair gives me freedom to apply that knowledge to her advantage and mine.

Hair Ignorance is not Bliss

Hair ignorance, whether intentional or inadvertent, is a problem. Ignorance about your *black* hair will cause you to make wrong hair choices that will lead to breakage and premature loss. Hair ignorance will cost you dearly. It cost you your hair honor yesterday, it is costing you your hair dignity today, and it will cost you your hairline tomorrow. You can no longer afford to continue in ignorance about your hair. You can no longer afford to base the knowledge of your hair on circumstances external to yourself alone.

Ignorance of the basic principles governing your hair have cost you hair leadership. You are not a "hair leader" but, rather, a "hair follower," hopping on the bandwagon of the latest hair fads that show no regard for your hair's delicate and tender nature. Your hair ignorance is costing you big time. Get rid of your hair ignorance. Get rid of it now. The only way to completely dispense with hair ignorance is to get educated. Yes, you need knowledge. You need knowledge about your hair and you need it now.

Hair Knowledge is Power

Hair knowledge is power. To know your hair is to know yourself. To know your hair is to understand her Source. Why is your hair the way she is? Why is she distinct, wavy, curly, coily, easily tangled? Why does she sometimes feel so coarse? What makes her soft and fluffy? What treatments make her shine? To begin to search out the answers to these questions, is to embark on an amazing lifetime journey of true hair knowledge.

True hair knowledge helps you understand the unique properties that define your hair and sets you free to pursue hairstyles that respect the individuality of your hair strands.

Knowledge of your hair helps you fight the pressure to conform to falsely accepted standards of beauty that do damage to your beloved hair and, in the end, limit her beauty and glory. Knowledge of your hair helps you define your operating boundaries. It tells you how far you can go, when to stop, and when enough is enough!

To get the knowledge you need, you will have to embark on your own personal hair journey. No, you will not be able to read about your hair in a book. You are unlikely to find the information you need on the Internet. You are going to need to pair up with a friend, call your sister, or find a hairstylist, and go on your own personal hair self-education expedition.

Get the Information you Need

To help you as you embark on your hair self-education project, I have developed a set of questions that you might want to use as a starting point for discovering more about your own hair. Take this list and use it to develop your own questions. Remember, the study of your hair is a life-long journey. You have so much to uncover about your hair. So, take your time to do it well. Some of the questions you should be asking are the following:

1. Where do my attitudes and thoughts about *black* hair come from?

2. What are the positive and negative feelings I have about my *black* hair?

3. What personal experiences have shaped my feelings about *black* hair?

4. Who is my primary *black* hair role model and why?

5. What are the variations in my hair texture?

7 Laws of black Hair

6. What is my dominant hair texture?

7. What products work best to add oils to my hair?

8. What products leave my hair feeling dry and fragile?

9. What is the optimal wash schedule for my hair?

10. What hairstyles suit my hair best?

Starting with the above 10 questions, you will gain some insight into the hair attitudes that drive your choices. And, you'll get to know your hair better. A better understanding of your hair will give you the tools you need to make the right choices that favor her.

black Hair is Misunderstood

As you embark on your journey of hair discovery and uncover new insights about your *black* hair, I hope you will take a minute to consider that you are unique. The uniqueness to which I refer is your personal knowledge of your own *black* hair.

Real knowledge about *black* hair is uncommon. There are over a billion people[1] in the world with *black* hair and most do not have the intimate knowledge of who she is and what she's about. Most people with *black* hair don't possess the basic knowledge required to take good care of her. Think about it: Many people have no clue about their underlying hair texture; some don't know what styles bring out the best in their hair; and some have no clue about how to style their own *black* hair.

To be fair, the journey to understanding your *black* hair is a lifetime endeavor. The journey can begin at any time. No matter how late you begin the journey, there is no shame. There is no blame. There is only celebration. Celebration at the possibility of what you are about to discover and uncover about your glorious, beautiful, *black* hair. As you go along your journey, you will discover many people who misunderstand *black* hair (fortunately, you will now no longer be one of them). The different ways in which *black* hair tends to be misunderstood are outlined as follows:

1. **Her form.** Why is *black* hair so big? Why does she grow upward and outward? Why won't *black* hair just lay low, stay out of sight, conform, be like everyone else? These questions are likely to arise from people who don't understand *black* hair's unique configuration. As we discussed in chapter 5, the Law of Moisture, *black* hair is different from other hair types. Her unusual form is simply a manifestation of who she is. *black* hair's big nature is consistent with how she was made. A lack of acceptance of her form does not change her in any way. You should be OK with her strange form. If other people are not, don't worry. Give them time, they will eventually come around, in this life or in the next.

2. **Her function**. People who stumble over *black* hair's function have a hard time because her function has historically been politicized.[3] There is a sense that, to wear *black* hair is to be political. No, politicking is not a function of *black* hair. I am not denying that *black* hair through the ages has been politicized. Rather, I am making the point that no one is born with political hair. The function of *black* hair is simply to beautify. The purpose of *black* hair is to make beautiful.

3. **Her tendencies.** People who struggle with *black* hair's tendency to coil, tangle, kink, twist, and knot, have in their hearts, a baseline view of hair that is eurocentric. If long, silky, European hair is the standard by which

hair is judged, then *black* hair does not conform to that standard. However, since neither European nor Asian hair is the standard, but rather God's hair, then *black* hair's tendencies are perfect, reflecting the tendencies of her Maker's hair – independent, strong, unique, special, royal, and just purely amazing.

4. **Her needs.** People who struggle with *black* hair's needs have no understanding of her underlying tendencies: Her thirsty roots must be watered; her tangled tresses tenderly caressed; her wayward knots carefully untwisted; and her dull persona lavished with oil. Again, see chapter 5, the Law of Moisture, to get a better sense of *black* hair's needs.

5. **Her desires.** People who struggle with *black* hair's desires struggle to accept that all hair is created equal in the eyes of their Maker. *black* hair, like all hair, longs to be welcomed, embraced, celebrated, and held in high esteem. *black* hair desires to be accepted on her own terms. She knows she is beautiful and she hopes that one day, all people will see it too.

Spread the Right Information

Information about *black* hair is unlikely to come from the dominant culture today. Perhaps, tomorrow, more positive information about *black* hair will exist in the mainstream media. But today, in your individual situation, the correct, more positive information is most likely to come from you. If it does not come from you, misinformation is likely to abound.

Try the following exercise. Choose your favorite search engine and clear out your browsing history and cookies. Do a search for "images" with the following search terms:

1. Hair

2. Professional hair

3. Unprofessional hair

When you do the search, what images come up? The images that you see likely reflect the dominant culture and may not adequately represent your *black* hair. If the images do represent your *black* hair type, they may not necessarily represent it in the best possible light.

Dispel Misinformation About *black* hair

The responsibility for providing information about your own hair type lies with you. You are the most reliable source of information that your world has about *black* hair. The only information your co-workers have about *black* hair is most likely to come from the *black*-haired people they encounter daily. If you are the only one, then it all rests with you. Don't discount the power you have to set the right expectations about *black* hair. If you have any sense of inferiority about your *black* hair, the world around you is likely to read your insecurities and reflect them back to you. Validation about your *black* hair and its inner beauty will not come from the world around you, it will only come from inside you.

Accept the Information Challenge

Your mission, should you choose to accept it, is to change the language around *black* hair by first changing your own language. Changing your language requires that you go and get truthful information about *black* hair. Only after you have acquired truthful information do you have permission to speak positively about *black* hair. I hope you will accept my challenge and go and get information that will empower you to speak up and speak out boldly about *black* hair.

The Law of Exposure

Exposure

What People Don't See, They Don't Know

The Law of Exposure

The Law of Exposure states that people become familiar with hair they are exposed to.

Definitions

The Merriam-Webster Dictionary defines "familiar" and "expose" in ways that are relevant to our discussion as follows:

Familiar[1]

1. Frequently seen or experienced.
2. Easily recognized.
3. Having personal or intimate knowledge.

Expose[2]

1. To make known.
2. To bring to light.
3. To cause to be visible or open to view.

From the above definitions, the Law of Exposure can be reworded as follows:

Hair becomes frequently seen or experienced, easily recognized, and people have personal or intimate knowledge of her when she is made known, brought to light, caused to be visible, or open to view.

She Thought I was Unstable

I started a new job a few years ago. At the time, I frequently wore my hair in shoulder-length hair extensions. In-between hairstyles, I would take out the extensions and wear my own natural hair. Wearing my natural hair to work provoked some interesting reactions from my colleagues. A coworker would look up and then look past me as if he didn't know me. Suddenly, he would look straight at me and exclaim in surprise, "Toyosi? I didn't recognize you. What did you do with your hair?" One colleague would ask, "You cut your hair again?" Another would say, "Wow! Your hair looks . . . different." I tried, unsuccessfully, to explain the difference between my natural hair and the extensions. But, no matter how carefully I explained it, I felt I was misunderstood.

One day, an older colleague targeted me for an "intervention." She sat me down and gently explained that she understood what I was going through. "What could I be going through?" I wondered, perplexed. She explained to me that, when she was about my age, she too, like me, had been unsure of herself and unclear about what she wanted out of life. She, like me, would frequently express her uncertainty in the way she wore her hair. She went on to explain that she kept changing her hair in search of the "right look" until she finally came to a point of understanding about herself. She eventually accepted herself for who she was. She felt that I had been experiencing the same kind of uncertainty about myself. And my uncertainty was being expressed in my constantly-changing hair. She assured me that, with time, I would find it in me to settle down into a look I liked. I would eventually "find" myself.

Wow! I was lost and somehow trying to "find" myself? Who knew? The confrontation took me completely by surprise. How was I to respond? She had been completely sincere. She really felt that I was experiencing inner turmoil that appeared to be manifesting itself in my changing hairstyles. She really did think I couldn't make up my mind about who I was and what I wanted. Every time my hair changed, she thought it somehow signaled some sort of instability. How many other people felt the way she did? What could I say? She was not being malicious; she was sincerely looking out for me. After a few moments spent collecting my thoughts, I smiled, thanked her, and walked away.

When They Don't See Your Real Hair

Perhaps you have had an experience similar to mine. You look amazing in your long extensions and glamorous weaves. Then, one day, you wear your natural hair to work and people don't seem to like the change. Instead of spending the workday being productive, you're agonizing over your colleagues' puzzling looks and quizzical reactions. "Do they hate my hair?" You wonder. Some people sincerely compliment you on your new do; but you don't believe them. You're caught up in the negative reactions of the others. You feel ugly and you think everyone sees you the same way. So you make a quick decision: You will not repeat this hair mistake again. Your natural hair will not be coming back with you tomorrow (at least, not publicly). But your hair appointment isn't for another 3 days? What do you do now? You decide, it's best to wear a wig. The next day, you don the wig and there appear to be sighs of relief all around. The old, "glamorous" you is back. All is right with the world again.

It's Not Them. It's You

If you have had a similar hair experience, know that the real tension lies, not externally, but internally. The real problem lies, not with your colleagues, but with you. You are the one who is presenting them with a new experience. You are presenting them with an experience of you that they are yet to become familiar with. Their response to you is an expression of a natural psychological phenomenon known as the familiarity principle.

The familiarity principle. The familiarity principle is a phenomenon by which you develop a preference for something just because you are continually exposed to it.[3] The more you are exposed to a new experience, the more familiar it becomes, and the more you gravitate towards it. Initially, with the new exposure comes a reaction of fear and avoidance. Over time, however, fear and avoidance disappear and you are able to approach the new experience with an open mind. The more you encounter the experience, the more you like it.

The familiarity principle applies to your hair. When it comes to a new hairstyle, the familiarity principle is at play. The first time you come in to work with the new hairdo, your coworkers are experiencing some discomfort because the look that you have presented them with is unfamiliar. Because it is unfamiliar, the initial response, especially for those who don't understand how your hair can change so dramatically, is one of fear and avoidance. But, the more they are exposed to the new look, the more familiar it becomes, and the more they like it. Given repeated exposures to your new hairstyle, your coworkers, now familiar with the new you, will gradually come to accept it as part of you and, ultimately, grow to love it.

Use the Familiarity Principle to Your Advantage.
Now that you are aware of the familiarity principle, you
can use it to your advantage. As you try it out, you can help
people come to know and love your real hair. Try it out in
the following 3 steps:

1. **Prepare yourself first.** The first person that must
   become comfortable with your own hair is you. If you
   feel uncertain about how you look and are hoping
   your coworkers will provide the external validation
   you need, think again: They don't understand it, they
   don't like it (yet), and, frankly, they wish the old you
   would come back. When it comes to validating your
   new appearance, you will have to look to yourself. So,
   get comfortable with and be accepting of yourself.
   Any negative feelings of inferiority or ugliness that are
   bubbling up inside you will be projected to others and
   reflected back to you. Get your inner-self right and
   prepared before you surprise anyone else with your
   "new" self.

2. **Be ready for the initial response.** Remember that,
   in line with the familiarity principle, the initial response
   to something unfamiliar is typically fear or aversion.
   When you experience the aversion, don't stumble over
   it. Give yourself time. Find a friend who will affirm you.
   If you have no such friend, look in a mirror and affirm
   yourself. Take a few minutes, take some deep breaths,
   and get over it. Go out into the office and introduce
   yourself again. Introduce yourself as many times as you
   have to; but don't get angry. Anger, in this situation, is
   unproductive and unlikely to win you any awards. Yes,
   there will be people that you feel are acting "ignorant."
   But give them time to get used to the new you.

3. **Repeat the exposure multiple times.** Now is the
    time to show up to all your company meetings, after-
    work parties, and weekend get-togethers. Come out
    of your cubicle or office space each day and say hello.
    Help your coworkers get repeated exposure to your
    new look, multiple times each day. And any time you
    run into a colleague who does a double-take when he
    sees you, target that person as someone you must search
    out and say hello to again that day. You will know your
    work is done when you walk into a room and don't get a
    surprise reaction from long-time colleagues.

"Is all this really necessary?" I hear you ask. You're right,
it's not. You don't have to go out of your way to explain
your hair to anyone. Your hair is your hair. You may wear it
the way you want and change it as many times as you like,
no questions asked. My goal in this exercise is simply to give
you a new perspective on what may be going on in your
coworkers' minds.

Some of them have no clue as to the ever-changing nature
of *black* hair. Some of them truly don't get it. Hey, some
people with *black* hair don't get it! In the earlier situation I
described, until she spoke up, I had no idea how confused
my older colleague was. People can be really clueless about
black hair. Help them catch a break. Exercising the concepts
behind the familiarity principle is a chance for you to give
your coworkers some "grace." You are not obligated to give
it; but I hope you will at least consider it.

Unprofessional Hair is a Myth
I'd like to burst a bubble about professional vs.
unprofessional hair. For the record, there is no such thing
as professional hair. Professionalism, as defined by the

Merriam-Webster dictionary, is "the conduct, aims, or qualities that mark a profession or a professional person."[4] So, professionalism has everything to do with the following:

1.   Your conduct – the way you behave

2.   Your aims – your aspirations

3.   Your qualities – your essential character

A professional image is one you project. You project the sum total of your outward appearance in the way you dress, the things you do, and the excellence you bring to the work place. Your hair can and should be part of that professional image. But, by herself, your hair does not equate with professionalism. Some people have a professional image but their outward behavior falls short of professionalism. Others have a professional demeanor and, no matter what they wear to work, they exude professionalism. It will be up to you to define how your *black* hair fits within your overall professional image.

Professionalism is not defined by your hair. Straight hair does not equate to professionalism. Most people who struggle with straight vs. natural hair as a marker of professionalism also struggle with hair identity issues themselves. In my experience, most of the people who complain the loudest about professional vs. unprofessional hair struggle with their own *black* hair identity. They wouldn't be caught dead wearing their hair a certain way and so they become the police to help everyone conform to their own personal image of themselves. If you look like them, you are OK. But if you don't, your professional image is suspect. While people with hair identity issues can't get over the appearance of "unprofessional hair," others mostly don't care.

Remember that there is no such thing as professional or unprofessional hair. There is only familiar and unfamiliar hair. The hair you deliver to your coworkers on a daily basis is the hair they will come to know and love. If you bring your competent, polished, skilled, and proficient self to work, then your hair is accepted as part of a truly professional image. The image you project is the only image they know.

How You Wear Your Hair is up to You

You get the final say about how you wear your hair. Nobody else gets to decide, but you. Not your boss, coworkers, siblings, mother, children, or significant other. No one gets to decide, but you. With this decision-making capacity comes the responsibility for how your hair is received. You also get to decide that. Should you decide that your hair is ugly or unprofessional, then guess what? Your perception will drive the impressions of those around you. How you view your hair determines how people will respond to her. So decide. If you decide that your hair is worthy of validation, then, good for you. Validate her yourself and don't look to someone else to do it for you. Don't look to someone else to tell you how to look. You decide and then help them get used to it. Expose them to your hair until they love her the way they love you.

Give Your Hair the Exposure She Needs

Your hair is an important part of your identity. But her identity is wrapped up in yours. Unless you accept her for who she is, then no one else will accept her. If it seems that people don't like her, look inside and ask yourself how you really feel about her. Take some time to work through your negative feelings and emotions. Discover where they come from and challenge your underlying beliefs and assumptions. Don't be a coward. Look your hair squarely in the face and tell her how you really feel about her. The problem is that she already knows. You may lie to yourself, but she is not fooled. She knows that it's not the world who has a problem with her. You're the one with the problem. You may blame everyone else but she knows it's you. And she can see right through your insincerity.

Until you accept your *black* hair, your every attempt to get the world to accept her will fail. Once you accept her, then you will be proud to introduce her to the rest of the world. And, as the world becomes familiar with her, they will come to know and love her as you love her.

The 7 Laws
Will Change
Your Life

Keeping the 7 Laws is a Personal Choice

In chapter one, we reviewed the importance of laws. The laws that govern your existence apply to you, whether or not you acknowledge them. Ignorance of the law is bliss until a law is broken and you face the consequences.

When it comes to your hair, the consequences of breaking the 7 Laws are personally experienced. The personal impact of hair breakage, hair loss, split ends, or scarred follicles cannot be shared by anyone but your future self. With no hair police on hand to arrest you, you are the only true enforcer of the 7 Laws.

Revisiting the 7 Laws

Let's revisit each of the 7 Laws of *black* Hair.

1. **The Law of Love.** When you actively show strong affection for and unselfish loyal and benevolent concern for the good of your hair, she will grow vigorously, develop successfully, flourish, and succeed. The Law of Love is the principal law. It is the law upon which all other laws depend. To keep this one law is to keep the entire law. Loving your hair will lead you to act in her best interests, meet her needs, protect her, and show her off. If you can only keep up with one law, the Law of Love is it.

2. **The Law of Investment.** When you put money into your hair and count your hair as a property in which money is invested, you will bring in profit from your labor and investment. The Law of Investment helps you define your hair goals and align your investments to match them. The Law of Investment helps you determine the price you pay to achieve your goals.

3. **The Law of Retention**. The key to your hair increasing in size, springing up, developing to maturity, and becoming increasingly acceptable or attractive is to keep her in possession or use, keep her in your pay or service, and hold her secure and intact. The Law of Retention helps you consider the principles that affect hair growth and helps you fight to retain the hair you grow daily.

4. **The Law of Moisture.** When a small amount of liquid is added to your hair to make it wet or moist, it prevents your hair from becoming easily broken, cracked, snapped, disrupted, overthrown, damaged, hurt, or offended. The Law of Moisture helps you understand the physical needs of *black* hair and helps you think about the choices you can make to help her thrive.

5. **The Law of Protection.** Your hair is deficient in physical vigor; not able to sustain or exert much weight, pressure, or strain; and not able to resist external force or withstand attack. Therefore, in order to maintain her status and integrity, she must be defended and shielded from exposure, injury, damage, and destruction. The Law of Protection helps you consider your *black* hair's weaknesses so that you can consciously protect them as you decide how to beautifully style your hair.

6. **The Law of Investigation.** One cannot grasp the meaning or reasonableness of, or be thoroughly familiar with, the character and propensities of hair that has not been observed by close examination or systematic inquiry. The Law of Investigation helps you to open up an inquiry into your hair's true self so that you can get to really know her and clear up any misconceptions you

have about her true nature.

7. **The Law of Exposure.** Hair becomes frequently
   seen or experienced, easily recognized, and people
   have personal or intimate knowledge of her when she
   is made known, brought to light, caused to be visible,
   or open to view. The Law of Exposure helps you make
   use of the familiarity principle to determine how to
   introduce your *black* hair to the world and help people
   get to know her as you do.

Make a Choice Today

You may notice that, throughout this book, I have stopped
short of telling you exactly what to do with your hair. I have
not told you to wear it natural, wear it straight, relax it,
texturize it, braid it, or use heat styling. I fully acknowledge
that there is no "one size fits all" approach to hair and I
respect the choices that you must make to fit your personal
circumstances and convictions. I hope that, by introducing
you to the 7 Laws, I have sparked a new, previously
unacknowledged, curiosity about your hair. I hope that you
will be pleased to initiate your own hair journey of sorts
and experience the adventure that is your *black* hair.

I hope that, as you continue on your hair journey, you will
at least consider different hair choices than the ones you
have made so far. As you exercise your hair options, stay
true to yourself and make choices that are consistent with
your values, hopes, aspirations, and dreams. My hope and
prayer for you is that you remain your 100% most beautiful
self, today and always.

black Hair is Beautiful

Their *black* Hair was Beautiful

During my childhood, my parents wore their *black* hair proudly. My father wore his hair in a big 'fro. I still have vivid images of the perfectly rounded, neatly squished 'fro he wore on his head. My mother also wore her hair in a 'fro; but it was a modified 'fro with the Jheri curl look of the '80s. She wore that afro Jheri curl look with a gorgeous smile. My mom was stunning. I would often spend time staring at her, thinking she was so beautiful. Her gorgeous afro was an important part of the beauty I aspired to.

Without intending to, my parents helped me cultivate an unwavering love for *black* hair. She went everywhere with them. When we lived in the United Kingdom and they were invited together to big international events, their *black* hair went with them. When they attended events where the Queen would be present, *black* hair went with them. When we hosted guests at our home, *black* hair was there too. *black* hair was always present. She was never hidden, never out of sight, always welcome, always on hand. She was an important member of our family and I grew up knowing that she is beautiful.

My parents unwittingly gave me a gift of *black* hair love. Because they loved *black* hair, I grew to love her too. Because they accepted her, without question, I accepted her too. She was a normal part of my childhood. As a child, I didn't have a chance to experience the shame or stigma that I see *black* hair wear now. I see now how lucky I was to have such a great early experience of *black* hair. My beautiful *black* hair experience is one I want to share with my children. My experience of *black* hair is one I want to share with the world. *black* hair is beautiful and everyone who gets to really know her falls in love with her beauty.

black Hair is Beautiful

What does it mean for *black* hair to be beautiful? It means that she is attractive, pretty, lovely, graceful, elegant, gorgeous, stunning, and magnificent. These words may not have immediately come to mind when you established your first impressions of *black* hair. In fact, you may still deny that they are associated with her. *black* hair? You wonder. Lovely, graceful, beautiful? No way! Yes way, *black* hair is beautiful. No, I am not kidding. No I am not drinking some kind of funky Kool-Aid. I am very serious. *black* hair is beautiful.

black hair is beautiful because the One who created her is beautiful. When He created *black* hair, He created it to look like His own hair. Yes, He did. He created all people in His image and His likeness. *black* hair looks like His hair. Don't be fooled by the dominant representation of hair in popular culture. Don't be discouraged by what people have said about *black* hair. Don't accept the lie you have been sold for generations. *black* hair is beautiful. Your *black* hair is beautiful.

Your *black* hair is Beautiful

Your *black* hair is beautiful. Your *black* hair is attractive, pretty, lovely, graceful, elegant, gorgeous, stunning, and magnificent. Your *black* hair may be the most important element of the amazing package that is you. Your *black* hair is beautiful, and you are beautiful.

I'd like you to go now and stand in front of a mirror. Put your hands on your hair and repeat the words of the following poem out loud:

7 Laws of black Hair

An Affirmation of my *black* Hair

My *black* hair is beautiful.
My *black* hair is beautiful.
Gracious and sweet,
Lovely and complete,
Pretty as can be.
My *black* hair is beautiful.

My *black* hair is stunning.
My *black* hair is stunning.
Luscious and attractive,
Divine and elegant,
Pleasing to the eye.
My *black* hair is stunning.

My *black* hair is magnificent.
My *black* hair is magnificent.
Glamorous and charming,
Delightful and appealing,
Graceful and revealing.
My *black* hair is magnificent.

My *black* hair is mine.
My *black* hair is mine.
Strong and glorious,
Gorgeous and alluring,
Fit for a queen.
My *black* hair is mine.

My *black* hair is beautiful.
My *black* hair is beautiful.
Gracious and sweet,
Lovely and complete,
Pretty as can be.
My *black* hair is beautiful.

I wrote the words of this poem especially for your *black* hair. I wrote it, so you would read it over and over again and keep saying it out loud until you truly believe it. You must believe it because it is true. Your *black* hair is beautiful, and you are beautiful.

Notes

Chapter 1: Your *black* Hair

1. Luke 7:36-40. *The Holy Bible*: New Living Translation. Wheaton, IL: Tyndale House Publishers, 2004.

2. John: 11:2. *The Holy Bible*: New King James Version. Nashville, TN: Thomas Nelson Publishers, 1982.

3. "Law." Merriam-Webster.com. 2018. https://www.merriam-webster.com (13 April 2018).

Chapter 2: The Law of Love

1. "Love." Merriam-Webster.com. 2018. https://www.merriam-webster.com (15 April 2018).

2. "Thrive." Merriam-Webster.com. 2018. https://www.merriam-webster.com (15 April 2018).

3. Deuteronomy 6:5; *The Holy Bible*: New King James Version. Nashville, TN: Thomas Nelson Publishers, 1982.

Chapter 3: The Law of Investment

1. "Investment." Merriam-Webster.com. 2018. https://www.merriam-webster.com (16 April 2018).

2. "Return." Merriam-Webster.com. 2018. https://www.merriam-webster.com (16 April 2018).

3. "Investment horizon." Investopedia.com. 2018. https://www.investopedia.com (16 April 2018).

4. "Dollar cost averaging." Investopedia.com. 2018. https://www.investopedia.com (16 April 2018).

5. "10 Tips: Build a Healthy Meal." Choosemyplate.gov. 2018. https://www.choosemyplate.gov/ten-tips-build-healthy-meal (16 April 2018).

6. "6 Reasons to Drink Water." WebMD.com. https://

www.webmd.com/diet/features/6-reasons-to-drink-water#1 (16 April 2018).

Chapter 4: The Law of Retention

1. "Grow." Merriam-Webster.com. 2018. https://www.merriam-webster.com (16 April 2018).

2. "Retain." Merriam-Webster.com. 2018. https://www.merriam-webster.com (16 April 2018).

3. Whiting DA. The structure of human hair follicle, Canfield Publishing, Fairfield, NJ 2004. Print.

4. Paus, R., and G. Cotsarelis. "The Biology of Hair Follicles." N Engl J Med 341.7 (1999): 491-7. Print.

5. Loussouarn, G., et al. "Diversity in Human Hair Growth, Diameter, Colour and Shape. An in Vivo Study on Young Adults from 24 Different Ethnic Groups Observed in the Five Continents." Eur J Dermatol 26.2 (2016): 144-54. Print.

6. Litt JZ. Litt's Pocketbook of Drug Eruptions and Interactions, 3rd ed, The Parthenon Publishing Group, New York 2004. Print

7. Deloche, C., et al. "Low Iron Stores: A Risk Factor for Excessive Hair Loss in Non-Menopausal Women." Eur J Dermatol 17.6 (2007): 507-12. Print.

8. Thom, E. "Stress and the Hair Growth Cycle: Cortisol-Induced Hair Growth Disruption." J Drugs Dermatol 15.8 (2016): 1001-4. Print.

9. Rudnicka, L., et al. "Hair Shafts in Trichoscopy: Clues for Diagnosis of Hair and Scalp Diseases." Dermatol Clin 31.4 (2013): 695-708. Print.

10. Mubki, T., et al. "Evaluation and Diagnosis of the Hair Loss Patient: Part Ii. Trichoscopic and Laboratory Evaluations." J Am Acad Dermatol 71.3 (2014): 431 e1-31

e11. Print

11. Mark 9:23; The Holy Bible. New Century Version; Thomas Nelson, 2005. Print.

Chapter 5: The Law of Moisture

1. "Moisture." Merriam-Webster.com. 2018. https://www. merriam-webster.com (16 April 2018).

2. "Brittle." Merriam-Webster.com. 2018. https://www. merriam-webster.com (16 April 2018).

3. Franbourg, A., et al. "Current Research on Ethnic Hair." J Am Acad Dermatol 48.6 Suppl (2003): S115-9. Print.

4. Tanus, A. "Black Women's Hair: The Main Scalp Dermatoses and Aesthetic Practices In." 90.4 (2015): 450-65. Print.

Chapter 6: The Law of Protection

1. "Weak." Merriam-Webster.com. 2018. https://www. merriam-webster.com (16 April 2018).

2. "Protect." Merriam-Webster.com. 2018. https://www. merriam-webster.com (16 April 2018).

3. Haskin, A., S. G. Kwatra, and C. Aguh. "Breaking the Cycle of Hair Breakage: Pearls for the Management of Acquired Trichorrhexis Nodosa." J Dermatolog Treat 28.4 (2017): 322-26. Print

4. Haskin, A., and C. Aguh. "All Hairstyles Are Not Created Equal: What the Dermatologist Needs to Know About Black Hairstyling Practices and the Risk of Traction Alopecia (Ta)." J Am Acad Dermatol 75.3 (2016): 606-11. Print.

5. Blattner, C., et al. "Central Centrifugal Cicatricial Alopecia." Indian Dermatol Online J 4.1 (2013): 50-1.

Print.

6. Tanus, A. "Black Women's Hair: The Main Scalp Dermatoses and Aesthetic Practices In." 90.4 (2015): 450-65. Print.

7. Richardson, V., et al. "Ten Pearls Every Dermatologist Should Know About the Appropriate Use of Relaxers." J Cosmet Dermatol 16.1 (2017): 9-11. Print.

Chapter 7: The Law of Investigation

1. "Investigate." Merriam-Webster.com. 2018. https://www.merriam-webster.com (17 April 2018).

2. "Understand." Merriam-Webster.com. 2018. https://www.merriam-webster.com (17 April 2018).

3. Saint Louis, Catherine. "Black Hair, Still Tangled in Politics." New York Times 26 Aug. 2009: 1. Print.

Chapter 8: The Law of Exposure

1. "Familiar." Merriam-Webster.com. 2018. https://www.merriam-webster.com (17 April 2018).

2. "Expose." Merriam-Webster.com. 2018. https://www.merriam-webster.com (17 April 2018).

3. Zajonc, R.B. (December 2001). "Mere Exposure: A Gateway to the Subliminal". Current Directions in Psychological Science. 10 (6): 224. Print.

4. "Professional." Merriam-Webster.com. 2018. https://www.merriam-webster.com (17 April 2018)

Chapter 9: The 7 Laws Will Change Your Life

1. World Population Prospects 2017: The 2017 Revision of World Population Prospects" https://esa.un.org/unpd/wpp. Retrieved April 23, 2018.

www.ingramcontent.com/pod-product-compliance
Lightning Source LLC
Chambersburg PA
CBHW021240090426
42740CB00006B/628